THE SUPER BOWL

Marlboro
Coca-Cola
NFL
RAIDERS

THE SUPER BOWL

ROLAND LAZENBY

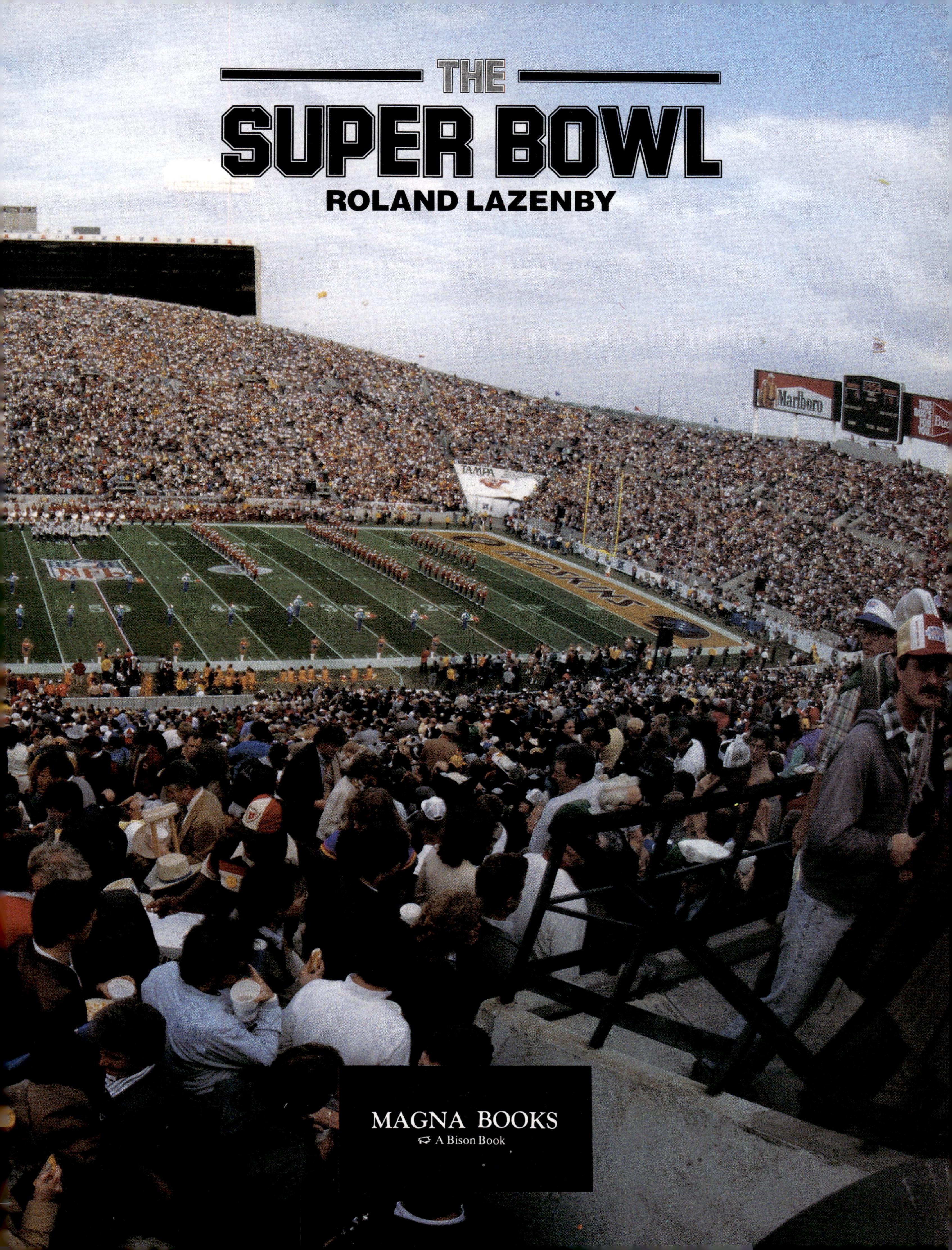

MAGNA BOOKS
A Bison Book

Published by Magna Books
Magna Road
Wigston
Leicester, LE8 2XH

Produced by Bison Books Ltd.
176 Old Brompton Road
London SW5
England

ISBN 0 948509 317

Printed in Hong Kong

Page 1: *Raider LB Rod Martin triumphantly holds the ball aloft in Super Bowl XVIII.*

Page 2-3: *Super Bowl XVIII's Tampa Stadium was one of only five one-time locations for the game.*

Page 4-5: *Super Bowl I: Green Bay's Willie Wood intercepts a pass from Kansas City's Len Dawson (16) and starts a 50-yard run to the Chiefs' four.*

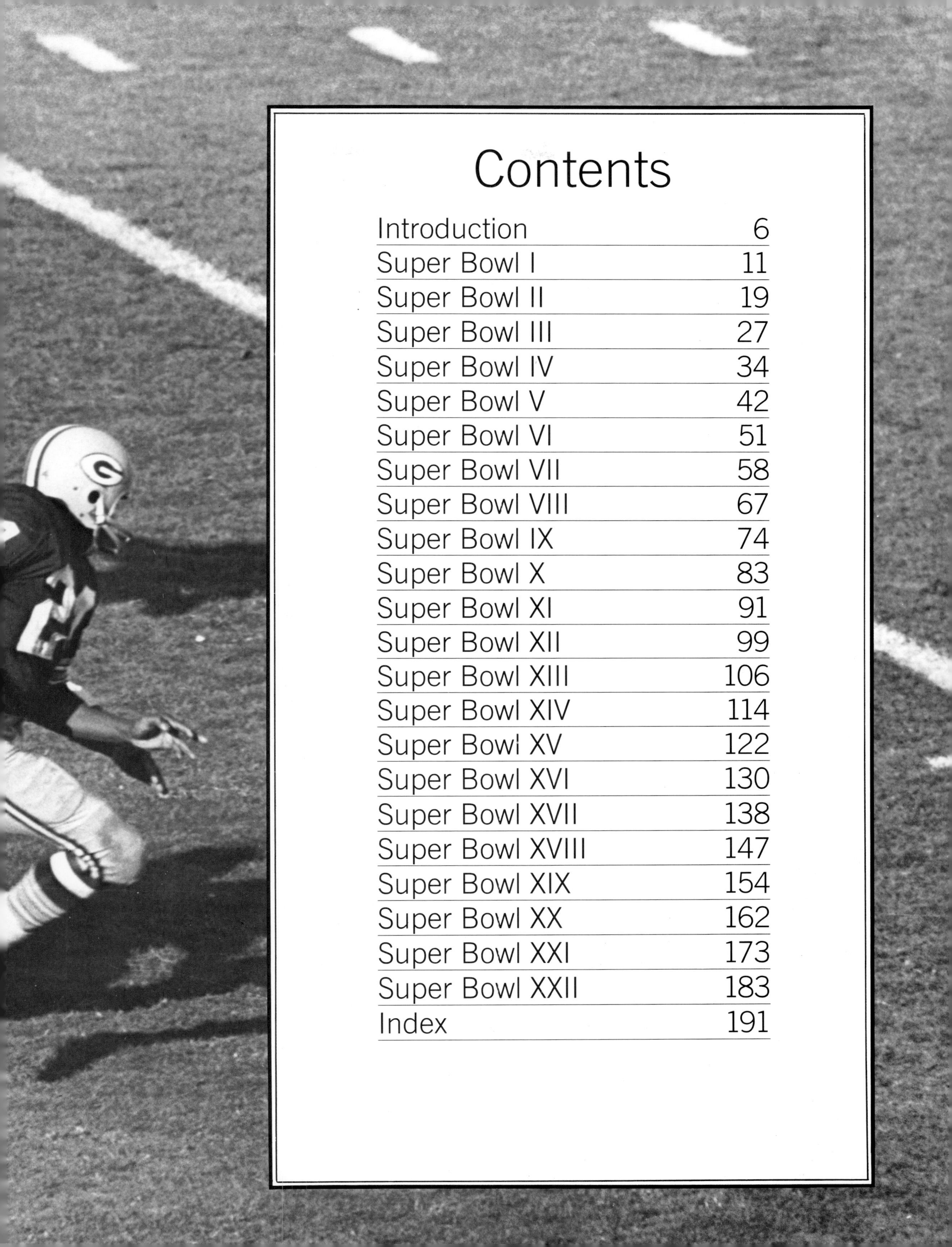

Contents

INTRODUCTION

More than any major American sports event, the Super Bowl is a child of the sixties, born in the turbulent decade. Most Americans, particularly the Baby Boomers, are intimately familiar with the setting. The nation was at war in Vietnam. Race riots and domestic violence ripped through New York, Los Angeles and dozens of other cities. The uproar of protest disrupted college campuses from the Ivy League to the PAC-8. Everywhere, the established order and the conservative values of the American past were being challenged by an unprecedented wave of liberalism and idealism.

Pro football couldn't escape this collision of values. The game's old order, the National Football League, was confronted by an awkward but bright adolescent, the American Football League. In an age when everything seemed so serious, this uprising in football was almost a mirthful, frivolous relief for the public.

The NFL might have avoided the hassle of competition if only it had been willing to expand a little faster. Ostensibly, the AFL was started because two Texas boys – Lamar Hunt of Dallas and Kenneth S 'Bud' Adams of Houston – couldn't persuade NFL owners to grant them franchises.

As with the half dozen rival leagues that had challenged the NFL over the previous four decades, the AFL initiated play in 1960 with a mix of castoffs, tired talents and second chancers. Here and there, amid the crowd of players, a nugget of legitimate big-league ability would glisten.

Whatever the individual assessments, the young teams made a beginning that year, and from it would grow a movement of style and savvy, a liberalism, that would eventually meld with the NFL, bringing the old league a new look, a new color, a new energy. The 1960 season brought a rush to get teams organized and games scheduled. For the snobs, the AFL was definitely a backlot league in those early days. Real football connoisseurs, however, knew a thrill when they felt it. If nothing else, these awkward young teams were entertaining. On occasion, they were even sophisticated.

ABC helped things tremendously by offering a five-year television contract worth nearly $9 million; it was the first trickle in a soon-to-be tide of media money aimed at promoting and developing professional football. So the bills, for the most part, were paid. And the teams, despite speculation to the contrary, survived.

As was expected, a bidding skirmish broke out immediately, the first fight coming over LSU's Heisman winner, Billy Cannon, who signed contracts with both Houston of the AFL and Los Angeles of the NFL. NFL commissioner Pete Rozelle challenged Cannon's plans to go with Houston, but the courts decided in Houston's favor.

In retrospect, NFL partisans might concede that the new league made great gains for pro football by opening markets in new places, such as Dallas, Denver, Oakland, Buffalo and Houston (the infestation would later spread to Miami, Kansas City and San Diego), or reestablishing a pro franchise in Boston.

The first AFL game, played that ninth of September, was considered something of an upset. But that's about all you could honestly say for it. Speed, power,

Above: *Unofficial symbol of the Super Bowl: the Goodyear blimp.*

Left: *Super Bowl XVIII's Vince Lombardi Trophy.*

Right, Above and Below: *Half-time hoopla: What would a Super Bowl be without it?*

precise blocking and crisp tackling – all were in short supply. Underdog Denver came back to defeat Boston, 13-10, with no-names such as Carmichael, Tripucka, Mingo and Colclough doing the scoring.

The premier team in the early AFL was Houston, with old NFL hand George Blanda flinging bombs. Bud Adams, the Houston president, had wanted a passing attack. Mac Speedie, the former Cleveland great who coached the Oilers' receivers, helped put one together. Charley Hennigan out of Northwest Louisiana developed into a great receiver. Teamed with him were two other prizes, Bill Groman and Johnny Carson. Cannon, out of the backfield, wasn't a bad target either. With that offense, Houston played its way to the championship game against Los Angeles in 1960. There the Oilers won, 24-16, when Cannon pulled in a Blanda aerial for an 88-yard TD to secure the victory. For good measure, the Oilers repeated as champions in 1961, nudging the Chargers, who had moved from Los Angeles to San Diego, 10-3. Adams, it seemed, had developed a powerhouse.

Before play had begun in 1960, the leagues had reached a verbal agreement not to steal each other's players. But Chicago Bears end Willard Dewveall found an avenue to the new league by playing out his option and joining the Oilers in January 1961. The

dislike between the two leagues grew, reaching a milestone of sorts in May 1962 when a federal court judge in Baltimore ruled against the antitrust suit filed by the AFL against the NFL.

If the AFL was going to make it, it would have to do so by generating excitement on the field. Fortunately, that had been little problem. The new league quickly established a reputation for gunslinging, with San Diego coach Sid Gillman leading the way with an innovative, wide-open passing attack. In 1960 the Chargers' Jack Kemp, who went on to fame as a conservative congressman and Republican presidential aspirant, broke the 3000-yard mark in a season of passing. He threw for 3018 yards in leading the Chargers to the title game.

Blanda quickly bettered that in 1961 with a whopping 3330 yards and 36 touchdown passes. He also threw 22 interceptions. The AFL's currency was thrill. Ultimately, it would have the effect of juicing up offenses throughout pro football. By 1963 YA Tittle of the New York Giants had thrown for over 3100 yards and equalled Blanda's 36 touchdown-pass mark.

For the AFL, the thrill image was epitomized in the 1962 championship game between the Oilers and the Dallas Texans. As with the pivotal 1958 NFL Championship between the Baltimore Colts and New York Giants, this one was played before a national television audience. And just like the 1958 game, this one went to sudden-death overtime. Make that *double* sudden-death overtime. Pro football's second championship tiebreaker lasted most of six periods, until Dallas placekicker Tommy Brooker nailed a 25-yarder with 2:54 left to give the Texans the title, 20-17.

For 1963, the major developments took place off the field. Lamar Hunt had moved his Dallas Texans to Kansas City and named them the Chiefs. A syndicate headed by Sonny Werblin had taken over the suffering New York Titans and renamed them the Jets. To bring more balance, the league allowed New York and Oakland to select players off other teams' rosters.

In 1964 things improved dramatically for the new league when ABC signed a five-year, $36 million television deal that would pay each franchise $900,000 per year. The all-important New York market showed signs of vitality as the Jets attracted a league-record crowd of 46,665 to their opening game in Shea Stadium, a 30-6 victory over Denver. The influx of television cash had allowed the Jets to draft and sign Alabama quarterback Joe Namath in the spring of 1964 for the unprecedented sum of $400,000.

As the adolescent league began showing signs of maturity, uneasiness increased in the NFL ranks. The 1966 season brought a whirlwind of competition, in and out of the stadium. Two new pieces were added to the board – Miami joined the AFL and Minnesota the NFL – as the leagues parried for television dollars. The ante was jumping. CBS paid $18.8 million for the right to broadcast NFL regular season games in 1966-67. That spring of 1966, the AFL and NFL handed out a total of $7 million to the top college draft choices. The beneficiaries of the mid-sixties spending spree were a few bonus baby rookies – namely Namath with his $400,000 contract, linebacker Tommy Nobis with $600,000 and running back Donny Anderson with $711,000 – a development that didn't sit well with established NFL stars, most of whom were making far less than $100,000.

The tension grew tighter when Al Davis, head coach and general manager of the Oakland Raiders, replaced Joe Foss as AFL commissioner in 1966. Swiftly, Davis dropped the agreement that the two leagues would not sign players off each other's

Left: *Super Bowl III: Despite a leaping Bubba Smith, Jet QB Joe Namath will launch his pass. The Jets beat the Colts in a 16-7 upset.*

Right: *Super Bowl VI: Dallas' Duane Thomas leaves behind a shoal of Miami Dolphins as he heads for the Cowboys' second TD. It was Dallas' game, 24-3.*

rosters. He targeted the NFL's low-paid veterans as the AFL's talent pool. Facing a bidding war that threatened to wreck both leagues, the NFL owners realized it was time for a merger.

In a series of meetings, the two leagues decided to become one with the 1970 season. Until then, the AFL and NFL decided to meet at the close of each season in a championship game, dubiously dubbed the Super Bowl. Lamar Hunt, one of the AFL founders, had come up with the name, reportedly after watching his daughter play with a Super Ball. 'I was just kidding at first when I mentioned the Super Bowl in meetings,' Hunt told reporters. 'But then the other owners started using it and the press started picking it up.'

Although it received wide popular use, that title wouldn't become official for a few years. Instead, league officials insisted that the game was the 'AFL-NFL World Championship Game.' So much for the official version. The words 'Super Bowl' were riding on the spirit of the times. In the climate of the irreverant sixties, a product had emerged, the Super Ball, full of vitality, able to bounce higher and zing off in different directions with a surprising vibrancy. To a degree, that was true of the Super Bowl, particularly in its formative years. But beyond its early drama and tension, the game itself has not always quite lived up to that name, at least not in the sense of a highly competitive, thrilling contest. A little more than a third of the 21 Super Bowls have been close or exciting. That, however, hasn't prevented the event itself, the extravaganza, from finding a home in the American psyche.

The Super Bowl in late January rides off the heels of Christmas. While the real thrill of the holiday often comes in the build-up and the celebrations beforehand, with Christmas itself somewhat less exciting, a similar fate has befallen the Super Bowl. The tension and the build-up of the playoffs lead us to the grand spectacle, where sometimes the big game itself cannot live up to its promise. But the game-day party atmosphere attests to the fact that for some, the Super Bowl is more a social event than a football game, and a thing of anticipation more than a thing of fulfillment.

It's important to note that the lack of sports tension and excitement hasn't dampened the public's enthusiasm for the event. The 1986 meeting of the Chicago Bears and New England Patriots was the most-viewed television program in the history of mankind, with an A C Nielsen-rated audience of 127 million. In addition, Super Bowl XX was broadcast to 59 foreign countries. The game itself, you may recall, was a 46-10 rout.

'The Super Bowl is world theater,' Marshall McLuhan, the late media genius, observed in 1969. 'The world is a happening. In the speed-up of the electronic age, we want things to happen. This offers us a mosaic that the fans love – everything is in action at once. . . . The games of every culture hold up a mirror of the culture.'

Historians in future centuries may look back in wonderment at our society's preoccupation with the Super Bowl. They may sift among the paraphernalia of the games, searching for a shred of meaning. The answer to their questions may be so simple that it will elude them. At its core, the Super Bowl is a championship football game. Nothing more, nothing less. One conference champion is trying to block better, tackle better and score more touchdowns than the other conference champion.

With that in mind, let us turn back to the volatile sixties, to the days of Vince Lombardi, when the old was being challenged by the young.

21
16

Super Bowl I

Green Bay Packers 35, Kansas City Chiefs 10

15 January 1967
Los Angeles Memorial Coliseum
Attendance: 61,946

Kansas	0	10	0	0	—	10
Green Bay	7	7	14	7	—	35

Green Bay – McGee, 37, pass from Starr (Chandler kick).
Kansas City – McClinton, 7, pass from Dawson (Mercer kick).
Green Bay – Taylor, 14, run (Chandler kick).
Kansas City – Field goal, 31, Mercer.
Green Bay – Pitts, 5, run (Chandler kick).
Green Bay – McGee, 13, pass from Starr (Chandler kick).
Green Bay – Pitts, 1, run (Chandler kick).

Rushing: *Kansas City* – Dawson, 3 for 24; Garrett, 6 for 17; McClinton, 6 for 16; Beathard, 1 for 14; Coan, 3 for 1. *Green Bay* – J Taylor, 16 for 53, 1 TD; Pitts, 11 for 45, 2 TD; D Anderson, 4 for 30; Grabowski, 2 for 2.
Passing: *Kansas City* – Dawson, 16 of 27 for 211, 1 TD, 1 int; Beathard, 1 of 5 for 17. *Green Bay* – Starr, 16 of 23 for 250, 2 TD, 1 int; Bratkowski, 0 of 1.
Receiving: *Kansas City* – Burford, 4 for 67; O Taylor, 4 for 57; Garrett, 3 for 28; McClinton, 2 for 34, 1 TD; Arbanas, 2 for 30; Carolan, 1 for 7; Coan, 1 for 5. *Green Bay* – McGee, 7 for 138, 2 TD; Dale, 4 for 59; Pitts, 2 for 32; Fleming, 2 for 22; J Taylor, 1 for –1.
Punting: *Kansas City* – Wilson, 7 for 45.3 average. *Green Bay* – Chandler, 3 for 43.3 average; D Anderson, 1 for 43.
Punt Returns: *Kansas City* – Garrett, 2 for 17; E Thomas, 1 for 2. *Green Bay* – D Anderson, 3 for 25; Wood, 1 for –2.
Kickoff Returns: *Kansas City* – Coan, 4 for 87; Garrett, 2 for 23. *Green Bay* – Adderley, 2 for 40; D Anderson, 1 for 25.
Interceptions: *Kansas City* – Mitchell, 1 for 0. *Green Bay* – Wood, 1 for 50.

QB Len Dawson of the Kansas City Chiefs in Super Bowl I. Dawson did well personally, but the Chiefs were no match for Vince Lombardi's Packers.

Above: *Packer fullback Jim Taylor (31) bursts through the Dallas line in the NFL title game, 1 January 1967.*

Inset: *Cowboy QB Don Meredith was one of the reasons the Packers nearly didn't make it to Super Bowl I.*

Left: *The Packers got off to a good start in the title game when Elijah Pitts (22) ran 32 yards for a TD. But by the last quarter Dallas trailed by only seven points.*

The Kansas City Chiefs and Green Bay Packers approached the first Super Bowl from entirely different perspectives in January 1967. For the Chiefs – for all of the American Football League – the championship matchup with the NFL was a moment for which they had waited seven years. In the board rooms, in the courtrooms, in the marketing strategy sessions, the new league had proved itself to be an equal of the old. Now it would have to begin proving that on the playing field.

'There will never be another single game to match this one,' Chiefs owner Lamar Hunt announced to reporters in the days preceding the game. To say the least, NFL executives didn't hold the same zeal for the event. The other side's strategic moves had forced them into a merger. Deep in their hearts, the NFL coaches and players felt they were facing an inferior football challenge. 'Maybe next year this will be the most important thing in the world,' Packers coach Vince Lombardi told reporters. 'But right now it isn't.'

If the NFL brass wanted a team to uphold the league's honor, Green Bay was the one to do it. The Packers were enjoying the zenith of their greatness under Lombardi. A former assistant coach with the New York Giants, Lombardi had taken over as Green Bay coach in 1959 when the franchise was mired in miserable losing. He made the Packers a winner in his first season, and coached them to the NFL title game the next season, where they lost a close one to the Philadelphia Eagles, 17-13. Over the next five seasons, Lombardi drove his team to three NFL titles, 1961, 1962 and 1965. In short time, he established a Packer tradition for intensity and toughness. His product was a mix of power and intelligence, burnished by his fierce temper.

Lombardi's teams were true dynasties loaded with talented athletes – Herb Adderley, Bart Starr, Jim Taylor, Max McGee, Carroll Dale, Paul Hornung, Forrest Gregg, Willie Davis, Ray Nitschke, Boyd Dowler, Jerry Kramer, Marv Fleming, Lee Roy Caffey, Willie Wood, Henry Jordan and many more. Even his players confessed they couldn't decide if the limelight shone brighter on their individual talents or on Lombardi's coaching.

After a brutal playoff game with the Baltimore Colts, the Packers claimed the 1965 NFL championship, 23-12, over the Cleveland Browns, and across the league, observers suspected that they were poised at the verge of greatness. While the upper division competition wasn't particularly close in 1966, the league offered greater balance. Deacon Jones and Merlin Olsen had given the Rams a Fearsome Foursome on the defensive front that helped lift Los Angeles from the league cellar into contention. Linebacker Dick Butkus had come into the league with Chicago in 1965, and while the Bears didn't win any championships, opposing offenses felt a certain dread playing against them.

The Packers rammed their way to another divisional title with a 12-2 regular season record. Bart Starr's passing spelled efficiency with 156 completions (a .622 completion percentage) and 14 touchdown passes against only three interceptions. His arm provided the perfect finesse for the Packers' sweep-oriented offense. 'Bart reads defenses so well now,' Lombardi said of his quarterback, 'that if the primary receiver is covered, he senses which of the other receivers should be free. Then he throws to that open man without hesitation.'

The main NFL challengers to Lombardi's troops were Tom Landry's Dallas Cowboys, led by the guile of quarterback Dandy Don Meredith, a slinger with enough poise to hinge a career on the two-minute drill, then graduate to Lipton Tea and Monday Night Football. The 'Bullet' in the Cowboys' offense was Bob Hayes, otherwise known as the world's fastest human. Meredith's other prime receivers were Lance Rentzel and Pete Gent, who would later author 'North Dallas Forty.' The running game moved on the legs of Walt Garrison, Dan Reeves and Don Perkins. Tackle Bob Lilly was the anchor of the defense that featured Lee Roy Jordan, Chuck Howley, Mel Renfro and Cornell Green.

A late-season, 31-30 victory over the Redskins and Dallas had its first playoff shot. The Cowboys were

just coming into their own as a franchise, finally lassoing the kind of success Texans had come to expect. But the promise of Tom Landry's first really good team evaporated in the NFL championship game before 74,152 witnesses in the Cotton Bowl, 1 January 1967, as the Packers scored twice to lead, 14-0, before the Cowboys had run one play. With Meredith passing and directing the ground game, the Cowboys answered with two touchdowns of their own to even things at 14 – all before the first quarter ended.

Starr reached Carroll Dale with a 51-yard bomb in the second quarter, and Dallas added a field goal by Danny Villaneuva before half. They pulled close with another field goal in the third. But then Starr drilled two more touchdown scores to Dowler and McGee. When the Cowboys blocked Don Chandler's conversion after the last touchdown, the Packers led, 34-20. Meredith quickly closed the gap to 34-27 with a 68-yard zinger to tight end Frank Clarke, and all Dallas needed was another chance for a tie game and a shot at overtime.

They got a second chance, and more, as Meredith drove them to a first down at the Packer two-yard line with time running out. The Packer defenders hunkered down, stopping Dan Reeves for a one-yard gain, but on the next play they received help from an unexpected source. Dallas was called offside, and the ball was set back at the six. Three straight passes failed, and the Packers were on the way to the first Super Bowl as 13-point favorites.

The Kansas City Chiefs had emerged from the AFL pack with an 11-2-1 record (by far the best in the

Left: *Pitts in action in the Super Bowl. Beyond him is end Max McGee, who made the Packer's first score.*

Left below: *The great Packer QB, Bart Starr, threw for 250 yards in Super Bowl I.*

Right: *The Packer defense brings down Kansas City FL Otis Taylor. The Chiefs only rushed 72 yards in the game.*

league) and thumped the defending champion Buffalo Bills 31-7 in the playoffs. They were quarterbacked by Len Dawson, and their defence was bolstered by a great linebacker, Bobby Bell, and a mammoth lineman, Buck Buchanan. Dawson had also run up some stellar passing numbers during the season, including 159 completions for 2527 yards and 26 touchdowns against 10 interceptions. He kept that pace in the AFL championship, completing 16 of 24 passing attempts for 227 yards and two touchdowns in the destruction of the Bills.

Still, the consensus was that Green Bay was much better. And nobody believed it more than Lombardi and his players. Sportswriters indulged themselves in massive pre-game speculation, focusing much of it on Kansas City's tremendous size advantage on the line. 'So what?' Lombardi retorted. 'We're also smaller than every other club in our league.'

For his part, Kansas City coach Hank Stram was contained and diplomatic in his remarks, saying only that the game would enable the fans to better evaluate the strength of the two leagues. What Stram lacked in braggadocio was made up by his players, particularly defensive back Fred Williamson, who called his clothesline tackling method 'The Hammer.' He offered the press opinions on Green Bay's players and said most weren't as good as AFL players.

To everybody's surprise, it was quite a game for a half. Although only 61,946 of the 100,000 seats in Los Angeles Memorial Coliseum were sold (at $5 to $12 each), the event had an audience – an estimated 60 million combined viewers from NBC and CBS, who would share broadcast rights for four years (a $9.5 million deal). A minute of advertising cost between $70,000 and $85,000. Plus there was plenty of outlandish pre-game and halftime entertainment, bands and dancers and batons and such. Somebody had the bright idea of releasing 4000 pigeons just before kick-off. Brent Musburger, then a Chicago sportswriter, had to clean pigeon droppings from his typewriter just as the game began. More than 1000 press passes were issued for the game.

The AFL official ball, which the Chiefs used on offense, was slightly more elongated than the NFL ball, which the Packers used on offense. The AFL's rule allowing a two-point conversion for running or throwing the point after touchdown was not in effect. Six officials – three from each league – worked the game.

If the play wasn't dazzling, the designers ensured the setting would be. The field was bordered in white, with alternating red and blue yardmarkers down the sidelines. The end zones were painted gold. At the center of the field was a combined logo of the AFL/NFL – in blue, red and yellow. The Packers dressed in their dark green, the Chiefs in white with red numerals.

For a while, the going proved just a bit tougher than the Packers thought it would be. Starr completed a 37-yard touchdown pass to McGee in the first quarter, and Green Bay led, 7-0. Dawson responded for the Chiefs by finishing off a 66-yard drive with a 7-yard pass to fullback Curtis McClinton. The Packers came back with a 64-yard bomb from Starr to

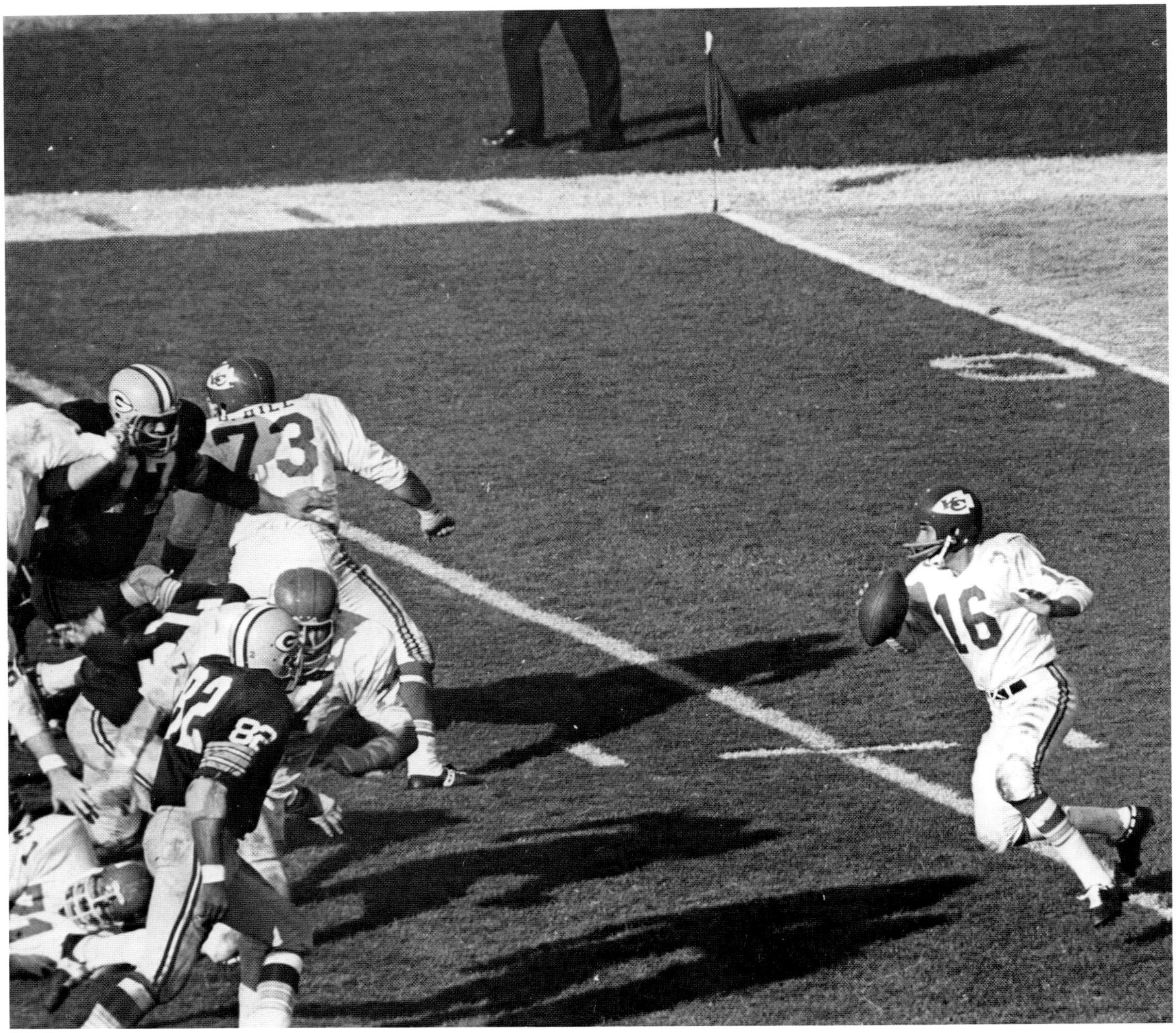

Dale, but it was called back on a motion penalty. Undeterred, the Packers continued their parade downfield, with Jim Taylor marshalling. He ran the ball in from 14 yards for a 14-7 lead.

Before the half, the Chiefs added a field goal and took to the locker room the hope that their youth would provide the winning stamina in the second half. The young league certainly had reasons for optimism, but the triumph would come later. The 1967 Super Bowl belonged to the Packers. Their experience, epitomized by their efficient ground game, prevailed. First, the Packer defense opened the half with the blitz that would sack Dawson three times. Even worse, it forced him to throw an interception to free safety Willie Wood, who returned the ball 50 yards to the Chiefs' five. Elijah Pitts ran the ball over on the next play, and Kansas City's hopes visibly sagged. From there, the Packers controlled the game with two sustained, time-consuming drives for scores. It ended, 35-10.

'I just wish we were in the same conference with Green Bay,' Kansas City's Buck Buchanan said afterward. 'We have people in our league just as good. I don't think we got disgraced. We just got beat.'

The winning players got $15,000 each, the losers $7500. Lombardi stood in the locker room afterward, tossing a ball from one hand to the other and answering reporters' questions. 'Kansas City is a good football team,' he said. 'But their team doesn't compare with the top National Football League teams.' Drawing attention to the ball, he said, 'The boys gave me the game ball. An NFL ball.'

Dawson and Stram agreed the key play in the game was Wood's interception and return. 'The interception did it,' Dawson said. Williamson, 'The Hammer,' sustained a mild concussion making a fourth quarter tackle and had little to say after the game. Teammate Jerry Mays summed up the game appropriately, 'The Packers and the Packer mystique beat us in the second half. . . . They beat the hell out of us.'

Regardless, this sports stepchild, the Super Bowl, had nestled in on the couch with 60 million television viewers. Even Vince Lombardi, the proudest of NFL guardians, realized that it had found a home.

Left: *Chiefs quarterback Len Dawson prepares to pass. In the game he completed 16 of 27 for 211 yards and one TD.*

Above: *Bart Starr (15) hands off to Packer FB Jim Taylor. Taylor was the game's leading rusher at 53 yards.*

Right: *KC coach Hank Stram being soaked with champagne after the Chiefs' win over the Buffalo Bills in the AFC title game, 1 January 1967.*

44

Super Bowl II

Green Bay Packers 33, Oakland Raiders 14

14 January 1968
Orange Bowl, Miami
Attendance: 75,546

Green Bay	3	13	10	7	—	33
Oakland	0	7	0	7	—	14

Green Bay – Field goal, 39, Chandler.
Green Bay – Field goal, 20, Chandler.
Green Bay – Dowler, 62, pass from Starr (Chandler kick).
Oakland – Miller, 23, pass from Lamonica (Blanda kick).
Green Bay – Field goal, 43, Chandler.
Green Bay – Anderson, 2, run (Chandler kick).
Green Bay – Field goal, 31, Chandler.
Green Bay – Adderley, 60, interception (Chandler kick).
Oakland – Miller, 23, pass from Lamonica (Blanda kick).

Rushing: *Green Bay* – Wilson, 17 for 62; Anderson, 14 for 48, 1 TD; Williams, 8 for 36; Starr, 1 for 14; Mercein, 1 for 0. *Oakland* – Dixon, 12 for 54; Todd, 2 for 37; Banaszak, 6 for 16.

Passing: *Green Bay* – Starr, 13 of 24 for 202, 1 TD. *Oakland* – Lamonica, 15 of 34 for 208, 2 TD, 1 int.

Receiving: *Green Bay* – Dale, 4 for 43; Fleming, 4 for 35; Anderson, 2 for 18; Dowler, 2 for 71, 1 TD; McGee, 1 for 35. *Oakland* – Miller, 5 for 84, 2 TD; Banaszak, 4 for 69; Cannon, 2 for 25; Biletnikoff, 2 for 10; Wells, 1 for 17; Dixon, 1 for 3.

Punting: *Green Bay* – Anderson, 6 for 39.0 average. *Oakland* – Eischeid, 6 for 44.

Punt Returns: *Green Bay* – Wood, 5 for 35. *Oakland* – Bird, 2 for 12.

Kickoff Returns: *Green Bay* – Adderley, 1 for 24; Williams, 1 for 18; Crutcher, 1 for 7. *Oakland* – Todd, 3 for 63; Grayson, 2 for 61; Hawkins, 1 for 3; Kocourek, 1 for 0, Kocourek lateraled to Grayson who returned 11 yards.

Interceptions: *Green Bay* – Adderley, 1 for 60, 1 TD. *Oakland* – None.

Packer RB Donny Anderson made a third-quarter TD in Green Bay's 33-14 rout of Oakland in Super Bowl II.

Far left: *Packer coach Vince Lombardi, after Green Bay's defeat of Dallas in the NFL Championship 'Ice Bowl' game, 31 December 1967.*

Left: *Green Bay guard Jerry Kramer winning the Most Courageous Athlete award, 29 January 1968.*

Bottom left: *Dallas QB Don Meredith (17) fumbling on a tackle in the 'Ice Bowl' game.*

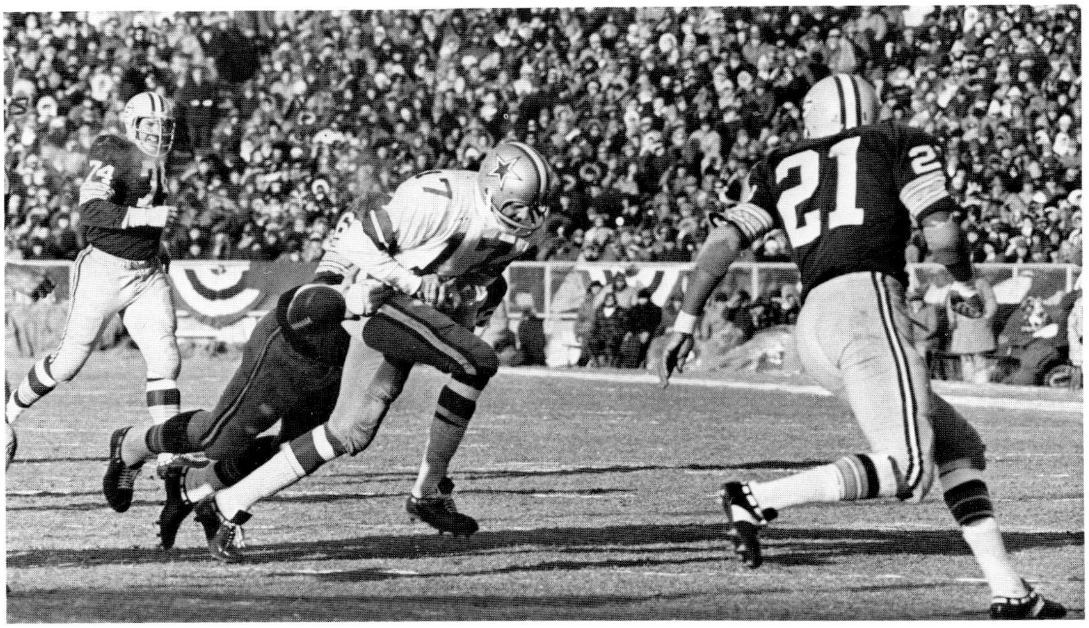

Top right: *Donny Anderson (44) runs through the Dallas line in the 'Ice Bowl' game.*

Bottom right: *Packer end Boyd Dowler scored twice on Starr passes in the first half of the 'Ice Bowl' game.*

If the football world hadn't quite grasped the concept over the previous six years, Vince Lombardi and his Green Bay Packers hammered it home in 1967 en route to Super Bowl II: *team*. The Packers were the ultimate football unit, drilled into a spare, precise machine, tempered by Lombardi's competitive fires.

The AFL asserted itself a bit in the 1967 preseason, as the Denver Broncos defeated the Detroit Lions, 13-7, giving the new league its first victory over an NFL team. Yet when the outcome mattered that season, Lombardi ascertained one last time that he was still the fierce protector of the NFL's pride. 'The pressures of losing are awful,' Lombardi once said. 'But the pressure of winning is even worse, infinitely worse, because it keeps on torturing you and torturing you.'

Earlier in the season, it had appeared that role of protector would fall to someone else. The Packers opened the season by tying the Lions, then over the course of the schedule lost games to Baltimore, Los Angeles, Pittsburgh and Minnesota to finish the regular schedule 9-4-1. The Rams and Colts, meanwhile, ran off impressive 11-1-2 records, with the Rams taking the Coastal Division title on points over Baltimore.

The Rams blasted the Colts 34-10 for the right to meet the Packers, the Central Division champions, in the Western Conference title game. But Green Bay ended the Rams' thoughts of greatness, 28-7, and began preparation to meet Dallas again for the NFL championship. The Cowboys had won the Eastern crown by humbling Cleveland, 52-14.

The 1967 NFL title game was probably the most frustrating in the short history of the Dallas franchise. Certainly it was the coldest. The game time temperature at Green Bay's Lambeau Field was 13 below zero, with a ferocious windchill factor that played as the Packers' arctic twelfth man. Lombardi was said to have prayed for a deep cold spell before the game. The answer to those prayers will forever be known as the Ice Bowl.

Green Bay management had installed 14 miles of heater cables six inches beneath the surface of the field to have it warm for the playoffs. But when the temperature dropped rapidly on the eve of the game, the warming system malfunctioned, leaving the damp field to freeze as slick as a glass pond. It was a truly miserable day for football. A little more than 50,000 fans suffered through four quarters of chill.

The scoring was as frozen as the weather until the early moments of the fourth quarter when the Cowboys took a 17-14 lead on a 50-yard halfback option

pass from Dan Reeves to Lance Rentzel. The weather Lombardi had prayed for was now lined up against him with the Dallas defense. The combination of the two worked to kill a Don Chandler field goal attempt minutes later. Then Don Meredith and the Dallas offense ran five minutes off the clock before punting to the Green Bay 32. There, with 4:54 on the clock, the Packers jumpstarted their offense. Between them and an unprecedented third NFL championship stood 68 yards, the cold, and one of football's best defenses.

Afterward, in the locker room, Packer guard Jerry Kramer recalled the mood in the huddle: 'Maybe this is the year we don't make it, that it all ends. But I know every guy made up his mind that if we were going down, we were going down trying.' In that frame of mind, the Packers started their last-ditch drive. First there was a six-yard gain by running back Donny Anderson. Then reserve running back Chuck Mercein sliced off tackle for a first down. Starr next threw to Bowd Dowler at the Dallas 42. Just as the momentum crested, the Cowboys threw Anderson for a nine-yard loss. Starr answered with two quick completions to Anderson for a first down at the 30, with 1:35 left. Mercein then got open beyond the linebackers on the left, and after Starr found him with a pass, raced to the 11, where he ran out of bounds to stop the clock. On the next play, Mercein dashed off tackle for eight yards to the three.

There, on a plane of ice, the two teams played out one of pro football's classic dramas. Two rushes by Anderson netted two yards and a first down. On third down and goal at the one with 0:16 left, Starr called for a dive between Kramer and center Ken Bowman. But rather than risk a handoff, Starr made the play a keeper. Said Kramer in the locker room later: 'He was going to go for the hole just inside me, just off my left shoulder. Kenny Bowman and I were supposed to move big Jethro Pugh out of the way. The ground was giving me trouble, the footing was bad down near the goal line, but I dug my cleats in, got a firm hold with my right foot, and we got down into position, and Bart called the hut signal. Jethro was on my inside shoulder, my left shoulder. I slammed into Jethro hard, coming off the ball as fast as I ever have in my life. All he had time to do was raise his left arm. He didn't even get it up all the way, and I charged into him. . . . With Bowman's help I moved him outside. . . . Bart churned into the opening and stretched and fell and landed over the goal line.'

The Packers had won their third straight NFL championship, 21-17, and turned their attention to the AFL's version of invincibility, the Oakland Raiders, who had finished the regular season 13-1, then obliterated the Houston Oilers, 40-7, in the title game. Coached by John Rauch and quarterbacked by Daryle Lamonica, the Raiders were rapidly building their roughneck image. Rookie Gene Upshaw and veteran Jim Otto were the nucleus of the offensive line. Pete Banaszak and Hewritt Dixon were the running backs, Fred Biletnikoff the primary receiver. Ben Davidson was the big name on defense.

The Raiders' Al Davis had acquired the six-foot-three, 218-pound Lamonica from the Buffalo Bills before the season. After serving as a backup for the Bills, Lamonica had come alive as a 26-year-old starter for the Raiders, completing 220 of 425 attempts for 3228 yards and 30 touchdowns against 20 interceptions, enough to win the AFL passing crown over Joe Namath, who had become the first pro quarterback to pass for more than 4000 yards in a season. But Oakland's real offensive weapons were its sweeps, led by mobile offensive linemen. The oddsmakers, however, weren't all that impressed and made the Packers 14-point favorites. Pity the fools who took the points.

The site was the Orange Bowl in Miami, and the crowd was a sell-out, 75,546. The pre-game ceremonies included two 30-foot-high figures, one of a Packer, the other a Raider, that chugged onto the field blowing smoke out their nostrils. Again, each league used its brand of football on offense. Again, the AFL rule for two-point conversions was not allowed. As the home team, the Raiders wore their

Above: *A happy Vince Lombardi watches the Packers score in Super Bowl II.*

Right: *Packer tight end Marv Flemming (81) runs a pass reception behind the blocking of Boyd Dowler.*

Far right: *Raider QB Daryle Lamonica passed for 208 yards in Super Bowl II.*

76
3

trademark black and silver. The Packers dressed in white.

As they had in Super Bowl I, the Packers won the toss and set to work immediately. Beginning on their own 34, the Packers drove to the Oakland 32, where the Raiders held, forcing Don Chandler to kick a 39-yard field goal.

Green Bay extended the lead in the second quarter by driving to another Chandler field goal, this one from 20 yards. Later in the period, Starr added another dash to Oakland's hopes with a 62-yard scoring pass to Boyd Dowler, who had slipped through a seam of confusion in the Raider secondary for a 13-0 lead. Facing an early blowout, the Raiders found their footing on the next possession, going 79 yards in nine plays. The scoring play was Lamonica's 23-yard pass to wide receiver Bill Miller behind Packer safety Tom Brown. As the half neared to a close, the Raiders were down only 13-7.

On the next series, the Oakland defense pinned the Packers deep in their territory, and for a brief instant the football world faced the illusion of a close game. Those hopes evaporated when Oakland's Rodger Bird fumbled the ensuing punt at his own 45 with 23 seconds left in the half. The Packers recovered, probed the Raiders with a few pass attempts, then settled for yet another Chandler field goal, this time for 43 yards, to stretch their lead to 16-7 at the half.

Starr dimmed the lights further in the third quarter with a long drive capped by Donny Anderson's two-yard run for a 23-7 lead. Then before the period ended, Chandler kicked his fourth field goal. Green Bay completed the rout in the fourth, when Herb Adderley intercepted a Lamonica pass and returned it 60 yards for a score. From there, the fans' hopes turned to Oakland beating the point spread. Lamonica managed another touchdown pass to Miller, but it ended after that, 33-14.

On the day, Starr had completed 13 of 24 for 202 yards and a touchdown. 'We made as few mistakes as possible,' he told reporters afterward. 'The game was very important to me. I felt I was representing every quarterback in the National Football League in this game, just as the Raiders were representing every player in their league. You play for everybody in this kind of game.'

The gate at the Super Bowl had generated an astounding $3 million, giving pro football's business managers an inkling of the gold mine they had happened upon. But the game was about to lose its biggest draw, the most prominent fixture of its first two years. The rumors had flown the week of the game that Lombardi was planning to retire. 'It's too early for such a decision,' Lombardi told reporters when asked about it. 'I'm going to give Vince Lombardi a real hard look.'

His players, however, played the game as if it was their coach's last. They knew something the public didn't. Weeks later, the team announced Lombardi had resigned as coach but would remain as general manager. That status lasted a year, until Lombardi was named coach, part owner and executive vice president of the Washington Redskins. He would coach

there one season before dying in September 1970, at age 57, of lung cancer.

His legacy would be a great one for the Super Bowl; for all of pro football. From 1959 to 1967, he coached the Packers to a 90-38-4 record with five NFL titles and two Super Bowl championships. To honor him, the league named its Super Bowl prize the Lombardi Trophy. In the modern age of pro football, the league's championship game may have acquired an air of hype, but at the core of its very spirit resides the granite substance of Vince Lombardi.

Far left: *Bart Starr, above, and Daryle Lamonica, below.*

Top: *Packer Don Chandler kicking a field goal.*

Above left: *Starr passing in the 'Ice Bowl' game.*

Above right: *Lamonica in the AFL championship game against the Houston Oilers.*

Left: *Super Bowl II: Packer Herb Adderley downs HB Pete Banaszak, causing a fumble.*

Super Bowl III

New York Jets 16, Baltimore Colts 7

12 January 1969
Orange Bowl, Miami
Attendance: 75,389

New York	0	7	6	3	—	16
Baltimore	0	0	0	7	—	7

New York – Snell, 4, run (Turner kick).
New York – Field goal, 32, Turner.
New York – Field goal, 30, Turner.
New York – Field goal, 9, Turner.
Baltimore – Hill, 1, run (Michaels kick).

Rushing: *New York* – Snell, 30 for 121, 1 TD; Boozer, 10 for 19; Mathis, 3 for 2. *Baltimore* – Matte, 11 for 116; Hill, 9 for 29, 1 TD; Unitas, 1 for 0; Morrall, 2 for –2.
Passing: *New York* – Namath, 17 of 28 for 206; Parilli, 0 of 1. *Baltimore* – Morrall, 6 of 17 for 71, 3 int; Unitas, 11 of 24 for 110, 1 int.
Receiving: *New York* – Sauer, 8 for 133; Snell, 4 for 40; Mathis, 3 for 20; Lammons, 2 for 13. *Baltimore* – Richardson, 6 for 58; Orr, 3 for 42; Mackey, 3 for 35; Matte, 2 for 30; Hill, 2 for 1; Mitchell, 1 for 15.
Punting: *New York* – Johnson, 4 for 38.8 average. *Baltimore* – Lee, 3 for 44.3.
Punt Returns: *New York* – Baird, 1 for 0. *Baltimore* – Brown, 4 for 34.
Kickoff Returns: *New York* – Christy, 1 for 25. *Baltimore* – Pearson, 2 for 59; Brown, 2 for 46.
Interceptions: *New York* – Beverly, 2 for 0; Hudson, 1 for 9; Sample, 1 for 0. *Baltimore* – None.

Super Bowl III. Baltimore end Tom Mitchell leaps for a pass.

The sports world had an excuse for being caught napping in 1969. The NFL had proven its superiority, and with the dominance of the Baltimore Colts during the 1968 regular season, the Super Bowl seemed a foregone conclusion. The AFL may have been enjoying its most entertaining year, with a sizzling Oakland Raiders-New York Jets rivalry. But the outcome was considered little more than a passing interest. Still, only an NFL snob could fail to take notice of the drama, with the camera focused on the brash, charismatic Jets quarterback, Broadway Joe Namath.

First there was the 'Heidi' game, the network gaffe that infuriated millions of television viewers but ultimately drew more attention to the raging competition in the AFL. Of course, Namath and the Jets were among the central characters, but they shared the lead with Daryle Lamonica and the perpetually dastardly Raiders. Aired by NBC, the November 17 matchup was a preview of the league championship. It was a darts match between Namath and Lamonica, an exchange of bull's-eyes featuring 71 passes and 19 penalties. Stretched by the style, the game was much longer than expected, developing into a 29-29 tie in the closing minutes. Then New York added a field goal for a 32-29 lead with a little over a minute left. Within seconds, Lamonica pitched the Raiders to the Jets' 43 for a thrilling close.

That's when NBC officials abruptly switched to a scheduled broadcast of 'Heidi,' the children's classic. Only viewers in the West, where it was 4 PM, were allowed to see the dramatic climax. Thousands of others in the East were outraged and immediately jammed NBC's switchboards with complaints. The network waited more than an hour to flash the outcome across the bottom of the screen: Oakland 43, New York 32. Lamonica had thrown a 43-yard scoring pass to Charlie Smith with 43 seconds left, then the Jets fumbled the kickoff and Preston Ridelhuber picked up the ball and scored again.

That scathing pace resumed 29 December in the AFC championship, played in the chill, swirling winds of New York's Shea Stadium. Oakland had gotten there by winning the Western division with a 12-2 record, then eliminating the Kansas City Chiefs, 41-6, in a playoff; the Jets had zipped the Eastern with 11 wins and 3 losses.

The weather grounded both air attacks early in the championship. But Namath used his favorite receiver, Don Maynard, to work on Oakland's rookie cornerback George Atkinson. Maynard beat Atkinson for a 14-yard touchdown pass in the first quarter, and a short time later, New York added a field goal for a 10-0 lead. Lamonica opened up the Raiders in the second period with a 29-yard scoring pass to Fred Biletnikoff, then Jim Turner's second field goal (he had kicked a pro record 34 field goals during the season) pushed New York a little further ahead, 13-7. George Blanda matched that moments later with a

Far left: *Incredibly, Jet QB Joe Namath got this pass off, but it was incomplete.*

Left: *Don Maynard, shown here in a game with Kansas City, was Namath's best receiver.*

Left below: *The Colts' RB Tom Matte (15) and QB Earl Morrall.*

Below: *Oakland Raider George Blanda kicking a field goal against the Jets in the AFC championship game.*

Raider field goal, and the Jets led, 13-10, at the half.

Another Blanda field goal evened the score at 13 in the third, but Namath pushed the Jets back into the lead with an 80-yard drive and a 20-yard scoring pass to tight end Pete Lammons. After Blanda kicked his third field goal to bring the Raiders within four, Namath resumed his attack on Atkinson. The Oakland corner responded with an interception and return to the New York five, setting up Oakland's go-ahead touchdown. Namath lashed back 30 seconds later with a bomb to Maynard at the Oakland six. On the next play, he threw again to Maynard in the

corner of the end zone for a 27-23 Jets lead. Lamonica had six minutes left to work some magic. His first effort died when he was sacked at the New York 26 on fourth and 10. The second effort took the Raiders to the Jets' 24, where a fumbled lateral ended Oakland's hopes.

The Jets were headed to the Super Bowl in Miami, but that didn't matter much, according to the pundits. The Baltimore Colts, with 15 wins against a single loss, were 18- to 23-point favorites. Johnny Unitas was slowed by injuries, leaving veteran Earl Morrall as the Colts' quarterback, but that seemed to make little difference as Baltimore humiliated Cleveland, 34-0, in the NFL championship. Morrall had replaced Unitas nicely, throwing for 169 yards against the Browns. Halfback Tom Matte was the heart of the Colts' ground game. He killed Cleveland by rushing for 88 and three touchdowns on the day.

But the Baltimore defense – anchored by defensive end Bubba Smith, linebacker Mike Curtis and cornerback Lenny Lyles – was the real foundation of the squad, and just about everyone figured it would make mincemeat of Super Joe and company. Which made Namath's mouthing off to the press in the days before the Super Bowl seem all the more preposterous. 'The Jets will win on Sunday,' he told the Miami Touchdown Club as he held a double scotch three days before the game. 'I guarantee it.' Later, he told reporters that Morrall wasn't as good as three or four AFL quarterbacks. Then he was reported to have told Colts defensive end Lou Michaels, 'We're going to beat the hell out of you.'

The Colts were a little taken aback by the woofing. 'All this Namath talk isn't going to fire us up,' grumbled Baltimore's Bubba Smith.

'Someday he'll learn a little humility,' the Colts' Billy Ray Smith said of the 25-year-old Namath. Few people listened to the young quarterback. The Colts were listed as 7-to-1 favorites, with the bookies giving 18-to-20 points to New York.

Opposite top left: *QB Johnny Unitas of the Colts.*

Opposite bottom: *Colt running back Tom Matte.*

Opposite right: *Jet cornerback John Sample, asprawl.*

Top: *Jet defensemen contain a Colt charge.*

Left: *Tom Matte goes down in front of back Alex Hawkins.*

Above: *Matte is snagged again by Jet LB Larry Grantham.*

The game had additional subplots. Weeb Ewbank, the New York coach, had directed Baltimore to world championships in 1958 and 1959, only to be let go after a .500 season in 1962. Baltimore coach Don Shula had been a defensive back on Ewbank's teams, and they shared thoughts on players. When Shula was ready to cut a promising young player, he would phone Ewbank and let him know. In fact four Jets – Winston Hill, Billy Baird, Bake Turner and Mark Smolinski – had come to New York via the Colts. Also, Johnny Sample, the firebrand in the Jets' secondary, had been traded by the Colts.

And, in a more restrained snobbish manner, the Colts matched Namath's talk with haughtiness. Club and network (NBC had paid $2.5 million for broadcast rights) officials began planning the victory celebration in the Baltimore locker room. Colts owner Carroll Rosenbloom went so far as to invite Ewbank to his victory party. The Colts, it's fair to say, played as they acted: fatly overconfident. Still, they were presented ample opportunity in the first half to make the game a blowout. But somehow they couldn't capitalize: It just wasn't in the stars.

Jammed with fans from New York and Baltimore,

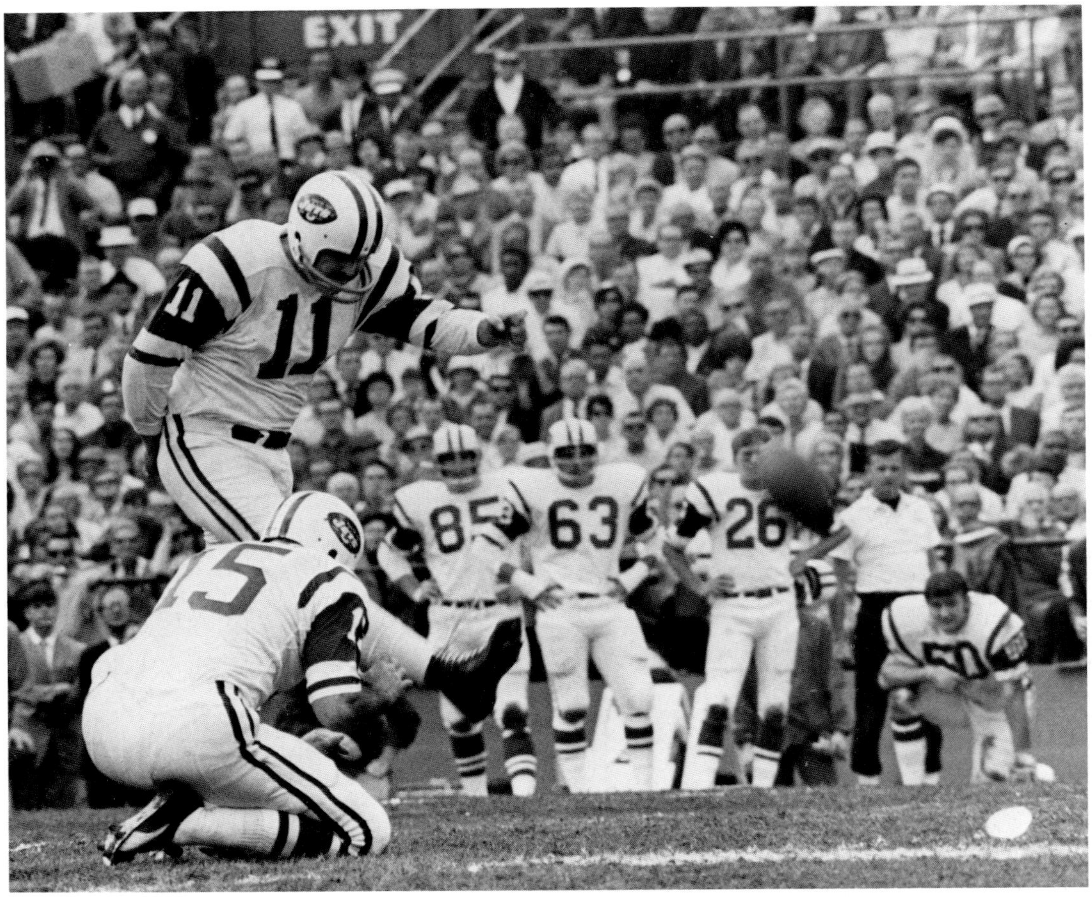

Left: *Jim Turner's three field goals gave the Jets their victory margin.*

Right: *Colt QB Earl Morrall gets off a pass as Jet right end Verlon Biggs closes in.*

Far right: *Jet end George Sauer snares a Namath pass.*

Right bottom: *Fullback Matt Snell scored the first Jet TD.*

the Orange Bowl was again a swirl of pageantry and color. For the first time, Super Bowl tickets were in such demand that scalpers made substantial profits by purchasing them at $12 and reselling them for $100 to $250 or more. The pre-game festivities included an appearance by the three astronauts who had circumnavigated the moon – Captain James A Lovell, Colonel Frank Borman and Lieutenant Colonel William A Anders.

The Jets received the opening kickoff and immediately established a ground game, with Matt Snell running effectively into the face of the Baltimore defense. The drive died after four minutes but it built New York's confidence. After a punt, the Colts promptly shoved their way down the field to a first down at the Jets' 19, where a pass was dropped and Michaels missed a 27-yard field goal. Moments later, George Sauer Jr fumbled on New York's 12, and the Colts had another chance. But Jets defensive back Randy Beverly intercepted a Morrall pass in the end zone.

The Baltimore defense was successful in shutting down Namath's primary target, Maynard, so he threw to Sauer instead, moving the Jets on an impressive drive to the Baltimore four. Snell then ran the ball in for a 7-0 lead. The Colts forged back, taking the ball to the Jets' 16 on the strength of a 58-yard run by Tom Matte. Again the Jets prevailed, this time with Sample getting the interception in the end zone.

The Colts returned to scoring position yet a fourth time just before the half, but Morrall failed to see wide open Jimmy Orr at the Jets' 10. Instead he threw to the other side of the field and suffered a third interception.

The second half opened with Unitas eager to play, but Colts coach Don Shula started Morrall again. Then Matte fumbled on the opening play, New York recovered and increased the lead to 10-0 on a Jim Turner field goal. After Morrall failed to move the team a second time, Shula inserted Unitas. But the Jets had shut down Baltimore's strong ground game and defended the pass ferociously. Meanwhile, Namath was troubled by a thumb injury and replaced by backup veteran Babe Parilli, who promptly took the Jets to another third quarter field goal and a 13-0 lead.

When Turner kicked yet another field goal two minutes into the fourth quarter for a 16-0 lead, the task for Baltimore and Unitas became nearly impossible. With four minutes left, Jerry Hill scored on a one-yard dive and the NFL's dominant team avoided a shutout. Namath, who had completed 17 of 28 passes for 206 yards, was named the game's Most Valuable Player. 'I always had confidence we would win,' he told reporters. 'But I didn't know what to expect. But I had a good time. When you go out and play football, you're supposed to have a good time.

'We didn't win on passing or running or defense,' Namath continued. 'We beat 'em in every phase of the game. If ever there was a world champion, this is it.' The Jets echoed their quarterback in chorus. 'We are a great team and this is the start of a new era,' Ewbank said. 'Ball control did it. We didn't make any errors. Joe Namath called a great game. He was fabulous, and he had great pass protection.'

Never at a loss for words, Sample couldn't resist the opportunity to gloat. 'We're the greatest team,' he told reporters. 'We put the Baltimore offense and defense to shame. When Earl Morrall released the ball, our defensive backs were racing to the ball. We read him pretty good.'

Assistant coach Walt Michaels attributed the upset to 'execution and great play by our safetymen. And I can't say enough about our linebackers. We sacrificed by letting the linebackers help out against passes. We didn't think their runners could go all the way. And they didn't.' Snell, the fullback, credited the offensive line with its straight-ahead blocking.

In the somber Colts locker room there was little question as to who did them in. The same Billy Ray Smith, who had said Namath would someday learn humility, could only offer praise for the Jets' quarterback. 'He did it all,' Smith said 'He threw the ball short a little. He threw the ball long a little. He ran the ball a little. He had it all going and so they won. I just couldn't quite get to him.'

Parilli, the Jets' veteran backup, agreed: 'He caught them off balance. He called the right play at the right time. He read the safety blitz and he read their pass coverage. What else is there?' Jet Larry Grantham had been with the team since its early AFL days as the New York Titans. 'We taught them out there,' he said with satisfaction. 'Now we're the first AFL team to be taken seriously.'

Namath reflected and told reporters, 'It was a long time coming, a long time coming for the league.' American victory would come again soon, much sooner than people thought possible.

Super Bowl IV

Kansas City Chiefs 23, Minnesota Vikings 7

11 January 1970
Tulane Stadium, New Orleans
Attendance: 80,562

Minnesota	0	0	7	0	—	7
Kansas City	3	13	7	0	—	23

Kansas City – Field goal, 48, Stenerud.
Kansas City – Field goal, 32, Stenerud.
Kansas City – Field goal, 25, Stenerud.
Kansas City – Garrett, 5, run (Stenerud kick).
Minnesota — Osborn, 4, run (Cox kick).
Kansas City – Taylor, 46, pass from Dawson (Stenerud kick).

Rushing: *Minnesota* – Brown, 6 for 26; Reed, 4 for 17; Osborn, 7 for 15, 1 TD; Kapp, 2 for 9. *Kansas City* – Garrett, 11 for 39, 1 TD; Pitts, 3 for 37; Hayes, 8 for 31; McVea, 12 for 26; Dawson, 3 for 11; Holmes, 5 for 7.
Passing: *Minnesota* – Kapp, 16 of 25 for 183, 2 int; Cuozzo, 1 of 3 for 16, 1 int. *Kansas City* – Dawson, 12 of 17 for 142, 1 TD, 1 int.
Receiving: *Minnesota* – Henderson, 7 for 111; Brown, 3 for 11; Beasley, 2 for 41; Reed, 2 for 16; Osborn, 2 for 11; Washington, 1 for 9. *Kansas City* – Taylor, 6 for 81, 1 TD; Pitts, 3 for 33; Garrett, 2 for 25; Hayes, 1 for 3.
Punting: *Minnesota* – Lee, 3 for 37 average. *Kansas City* – Wilson, 4 for 48.5.
Punt Returns: *Minnesota* – West, 2 for 18. *Kansas City* – Garrett, 1 for 0.
Kickoff Returns: *Minnesota* – West, 3 for 46; Jones, 1 for 33. *Kansas City* – Hayes, 2 for 36.
Interceptions: *Minnesota* – Krause, 1 for 0. *Kansas City* – Lanier, 1 for 9; Robinson, 1 for 9; Thomas, 1 for 6.

Minnesota running back Bill Brown runs for daylight in Super Bowl IV.

NFL
30

Left: *A Viking bags Kansas City RB Robert Holmes, whose five carries gained but seven yards for the Chiefs.*

Above: *Linebacker Bobby Bell, one of the stars of the famed Kansas City defense.*

After previous stops in Los Angeles and Miami, the Super Bowl settled into the music and smoke of New Orleans in January 1970. But instead of a jazzy championship, pro football fans were treated to a bare-knuckles barroom brawl. And as it had the year before, the American Football League threw the knock-out punches.

If the fans thought the AFL's Super Bowl III victory was a fluke, the Kansas City Chiefs shoved reality in their faces with a convincing 23-7 win over the Minnesota Vikings in Super Bowl IV. And the Chiefs were a second-place finisher in the AFL regular season standings. The league had adopted a crossover playoff system, allowing the runner-up of one division to play the champion of the other. The Chiefs rode that rule to glory in 1969 after finishing the regular season. Joe Namath and the Jets won the AFL's Eastern Division, only to be knocked out of the playoffs by Kansas City, 13-6. The Chiefs' offense was guided by quarterback Len Dawson and bolstered by veteran placekicker Jan Stenerud. Mike Garrett gave the ground game its wheels. The defense, with Curley Culp, Buck Buchanan, Bobby Bell and Willie Lanier, was already renowned.

Oakland, with a 12-1-1 record, had been the AFL's dominant team and had already beaten the Chiefs twice during the regular season. Things appeared no different in the championship game when the Raiders drove to a first quarter touchdown and a 7-0 lead. But Dawson and the offense finally found a seam in the Oakland defense in the second quarter and tied the game at 7. In the second half, the Kansas City defense took over, gleaning four Raider passes from the skies and creating opportunity for the offense. The Chiefs scored on a third-quarter drive, a five-yard run by Robert Holmes, then Stenerud kicked a fourth quarter field goal, enough for a 17-7 upset, making the Chiefs the precursor of a wild-card wonder.

Suddenly, the second-place team was headed for the Super Bowl. Their big names didn't stop the Chiefs from being 13-point underdogs to swashbuckling Joe Kapp and the Minnesota Vikings, who had hammered their way to the NFL championship. Kapp was described as a mediocre passer, yet he had thrown a record-tying seven touchdown passes in demolishing the defending-champion Colts, 52-14, early in the season. More than their offense, coach

Left top: *The Chiefs' Jan Stenerud (3) kicked a 48-yard field goal in the first quarter. He made three FGs and two extra points in the game.*

Above: *Teammates congratulate Mike Garrett, who made KC's first TD of the game.*

Left: *Viking QB Joe Kapp gets off a pass before monster 287-pound KC tackle Buck Buchanan (86) can fall on him.*

Bud Grant's Vikings were known for defense. Carl Eller, Jim Marshall, Alan Page and Gary Larsen made a very mean front four. After edging Los Angeles, 23-20, for the Western Conference title, the Vikings met the Cleveland Browns for the NFL championship.The Browns with Bill Nelsen at quarterback had eradicated Dallas, 38-14, to win the East. The NFL title game was played in Bloomington in the heart of January in eight-degree weather. Blowing frosty clouds of breath, the Vikings relished the cold. Kapp ran for one touchdown and passed for another in the first quarter as Minnesota raced out to a 14-0 lead and never stopped. By the third quarter, it was 27-0. The Browns scored late in the game to finish, 27-7, a margin that erased any doubt that the Vikings were for real.

The site of Super Bowl IV was Tulane Stadium, but the item of hype quickly became Dawson. He had labored for eight seasons in the AFL, throwing 192 touchdown passes in that time, more than any other-pro quarterback. In 1969 he had missed six games with a knee injury, suffered through the death of his father, and then had to weather a storm of criticism about his play. On the eve of Super Bowl IV, just when it seemed he had put those things behind him, Dawson, Joe Namath and two other pro quarterbacks were implicated in a news story about a federal gambling investigation. The error of the story was later revealed, but in the heat of the moment Dawson's teammates and coach Hank Stram rallied around him. If the Chiefs hadn't had a sense of purpose, the press helped them find one. 'We're angry as hell the story came out like it did,' Kansas City's Jerry Mays told reporters.

The Vikings, on the other hand, were happy to let their pre-game hype center on Kapp's rough-and-tumble image. Much of that stemmed from an anecdote about Kapp's barroom fight with Minnesota linebacker Lonnie Warwick. Kapp, it seems, wanted to blame a Vikings' loss on his fumble. Warwick, on the other hand, said the defense was at fault because it gave up too many points. Unable to reach an agreement, the two decided to settle it outside. Warwick decked Kapp with a shot to the left eye, but the quarterback's readiness to fight impressed his teammates. Kapp couldn't throw, couldn't run, but he sure could battle. Born of German and Mexican parents, Kapp was raised in California and went on to star at the University of California, where he earned All-America honors. He was drafted in the eighteenth round by the Washington Redskins in 1959, but elected to play in the Canadian Football League. Grant, a former Canadian League coach, was only too happy to acquire Kapp in 1967. Grant believed in the thoery that big plays turn the tide of football games, and that the best players were always poised to make them when opportunity allowed. Kapp, it seemed, was a big-play quarterback.

Above: *Minnesota's tough Joe Kapp was a more inspirational than skillful leader.*

Right: *Safety Johnny Robinson of the powerful KC defense.*

Right top: *QB Len Dawson (16) huddles with the KC offense. Among others visible: backs Wendell Hayes (38) and Mike Garrett (21) and wide receiver Otis Taylor (89).*

Along with the gambling cloud over Dawson, the Chiefs were trying to move away from their record as a big loser in Super Bowl I. 'The Chiefs,' Kansas City owner Lamar Hunt told reporters, 'are much improved over the team that lost to Green Bay. We have seven new starters on defense.'

In the three seasons since Super Bowl I, Kansas City had played nine pre-season games against NFL teams and won seven of them. 'The mystery is gone as far as the NFL is concerned,' Dawson said. The Chiefs may have believed it, but few others did. Oddsmakers set the spread at 13 points. The prospect of a blowout didn't seem to deter the fans, as all 80,997 tickets were sold at $15 each.

To make sure the fans wouldn't go wanting for entertainment, Super Bowl organizers booked opera

singer Marguerite Piazza to sing 'Basin Street Blues' at halftime. Doc Severinsen, the television trumpet man, played the National Anthem honors as actor Pat O'Brien recited the words. Also scheduled to appear were astronauts Neil Armstrong and Edwin Aldrin and baseball great Stan Musial. For good measure, the ceremonies also called for the release of 3000 pigeons, the shooting of fireworks and a re-enactment of the Battle of New Orleans. New Orleans residents viewed the entire event as a good tune-up for the Mardi Gras, set to hit town just weeks after the Super Bowl. Their main embarrassment was the weather. The temperature dropped into the low twenties in the days before the game, then a cold rain began falling the day before. It ceased at noon on game day, and the mercury moved to the sixties.

Kansas City's strength was supposed to be its defense, but the offense did its work early. Stenerud came on to kick three field goals. After the third field goal, Minnesota's Charlie West fumbled the kickoff at his 19, where the Chiefs recovered. Moments later, Garrett scored a five-yard touchdown run behind a block from Mo Moorman to give the Chiefs a 16-0 halftime lead, the same margin that had worked so well for the Jets a year earlier.

It proved just as safe for the Chiefs, who rode their defense and ball control in the second half. 'When we came in at the half, we knew there were only 30 minutes left,' Dawson said later. 'We wanted to keep our composure. We wanted to make sure we didn't give away anything and we didn't.'

Throughout the first half, the Vikings had crossed midfield only twice, each time without threatening. They made only four first downs. Things didn't improve much in the second. The Chiefs controlled the ball for the first six minutes. But then the Vikings sustained a drive, with Dave Osborn scoring on a four-yard run to close the score to 16-7. The Chiefs seemed stalled at third and long at their own 32 on the next possession. There, Dawson crossed up the Viking defense with a flanker reverse instead of a pass. Flanker Frank Pitts carried for a first down (on the day he would run the play three times for 37 yards). The Vikings, accused of roughing Dawson throughout the game, were penalized 15 yards for roughing the passer after that. From the Minnesota 46, Dawson zipped a touchdown strike to Otis Taylor, giving the Chiefs a 23-7 lead.

Harried and forced to play catch up, Kapp threw two interceptions in the fourth quarter before being knocked from the game with an injured shoulder with four minutes left. His backup, Gary Cuozzo, also threw an interception, as the Chiefs preserved their margin. The hard feelings between the two teams were evidenced by the battering delivered to the quarterbacks.

Far left: *Viking CB Earsell Mackbee stops Otis Taylor. Receiver Taylor caught six for a total of 81 yards.*

Left: *Chiefs QB Len Dawson. He played the game under a cloud of suspicion raised by a news story that erroneously linked him to gambling.*

Below: *KC's Mike Garrett led the game's stats in rushing: 39 yards. He added another 29 yards receiving.*

Right: *Chiefs coach Hank Stram proudly displays the trophy his team won in Super Bowl IV.*

Dawson was the first Chief into the locker room, where he faced an immediate barrage of questions about the effect of the gambling allegations on his play. 'The entire week was quite an ordeal for me,' he said. 'But I didn't win the game, the whole team did.' He had completed 12 of 17 passes for 142 yards with one interception and one touchdown. In addition, he had scrambled once for 11 yards. President Richard Nixon phoned his congratulations to Dawson in the locker room. The quarterback plugged his ear and attempted to hear the President. 'He told us we did a great job and said the youth of the world looks up to pro players for courage,' Dawson explained to reporters. 'I told him we try to exemplify what is good in professional football.'

Finally, the spotlight had settled on the reserved 34-year-old Dawson, the Purdue All-American who had been cut from the NFL after playing five years for Cleveland and Pittsburgh. 'It's a great thing, especially for Len Dawson,' Chiefs owner Lamar Hunt said of the victory. 'What happened earlier in the week put a great deal of pressure on him, and he proved that he's one of the great quarterbacks in pro football. He has been called a castoff because two National Football League teams didn't want him, but now he should finally get the recognition he deserves.'

Asked for his comments, Minnesota coach Bud Grant replied, 'We played a great football team. They beat us. It's as simple as that. They came up with the big play, didn't fumble, moved the ball when they had to and were not hurt by the interception. They just beat us with fine personnel. No secrets. We put our best on the line. They put their best on the line, and they were a better football team . . . today.'

Viking defensive end Carl Eller identified the second quarter touchdown after the kickoff fumble as the turning point. 'When they got that touchdown, that put them three scores out,' he said. 'That's what changed the game.' The victory also threw the spotlight on Hank Stram, the Chiefs' fireplug of a coach. 'In his own way,' observed a Chiefs official, 'he is just as tough as Vince Lombardi. If Lombardi does it with a hammer, Hank does it with a velvet hammer.'

Around the country, the AFL owners were smiling. They were ready to merge with the NFL, and evening up their Super Bowl record with the older league made the change that much easier. It also didn't hurt that the Super Bowl gate was another record, $3.8 million. Asked to reflect on the first decade of the AFL, Lamar Hunt paused. 'It's been a lot of fun,' he said. 'I don't care who started it, but it's nice that the Chiefs finished it.'

Super Bowl V

Baltimore Colts 16, Dallas Cowboys 13

17 January 1971
Orange Bowl, Miami
Attendance: 79,204

Baltimore	0	6	0	10	—	16
Dallas	3	10	0	0	—	13

Dallas – Field goal, 14, Clark.
Dallas – Field goal, 30, Clark.
Baltimore – Mackey, 75, pass from Unitas (kick blocked).
Dallas – Thomas, 7, pass from Morton (Clark kick).
Baltimore – Nowatzke, 2, run (O'Brien kick).
Baltimore – Field goal, 32, O'Brien.

Rushing: *Baltimore* – Nowatzke, 10 for 33, 1 TD; Bulaich, 18 for 28; Unitas, 1 for 4; Havrilak, 1 for 3; Morrall, 1 for 1. *Dallas* – Garrison, 12 for 65; Thomas, 18 for 35; Morton, 1 for 2.
Passing: *Baltimore* – Unitas, 3 of 9 for 88, 1 TD, 2 int; Morrall, 7 of 15 for 147, 1 int; Havrilak, 1 of 1 for 25. *Dallas* – Morton, 12 of 26 for 127, 1 TD, 3 int.
Receiving: *Baltimore* – Jefferson, 3 for 52; Mackey, 2 for 80, 1 TD; Hinton, 2 for 51; Havrilak, 2 for 27; Nowatzke, 1 for 45; Bulaich, 1 for 5. *Dallas* – Reeves, 5 for 46; Thomas, 4 for 21, 1 TD; Garrison, 2 for 19; Hayes, 1 for 41.
Punting: *Baltimore* – Lee, 4 for 41.5 average. *Dallas* – Widby, 9 for 41.9.
Punt Returns: *Baltimore* – Logan, 1 for 8; Gardin, 4 for 4. *Dallas* – Hayes, 3 for 9.
Kickoff Returns: *Baltimore* – Duncan, 4 for 90. *Dallas* – Harris, 1 for 18; Hill, 1 for 14; Kiner, 1 for 2.
Interceptions: *Baltimore* – Volk, 1 for 30; Logan, 1 for 14; Curtis, 1 for 13. *Dallas* – Howley, 2 for 22; Renfro, 1 for 0.

Super Bowl V. Cowboy RB Walt Garrison, the game's leading rusher, is downed by a mob of Baltimore defensemen.

Above: *Colts QB Earl Morrall gets set to pass while guard John Williams blocks for him.*

Right: *Dallas' Craig Morton (14) replaced Johnny Unitas at QB for much of the game.*

Far right: *Morton gets off a pass just in time. The game was marked by 11 fumbles and interceptions and 14 penalties. Baltimore led in turnovers, Dallas in penalties, hence the derisive name 'Blooper Bowl.'*

Super Bowl V hangs in the American memory as 'the Blooper Bowl,' a game rife with turnovers and freak plays. At least that was the media reaction in the aftermath of the Baltimore Colts' last-second 16-13 victory over the Dallas Cowboys. Yet, for the most part, the game was little more than an old-fashioned defensive struggle. Rather than a Super Bowl, it had the tone of an NFL title game. The AFL/NFL merger was officially consummated with the 1970 season, lending a tentative, uncertain atmosphere to the competition that fall.

Finally, after struggling early in the season, the Colts and Cowboys emerged to take the respective championships of the newly formed American Football Conference and National Football Conference. Led by quarterback Craig Morton (with Roger Staubach waiting in the wings) and mercurial rookie running back Duane Thomas, the Cowboys had been projected as division champions with a good shot at making the Super Bowl. But by mid-November, they were 5-3 and heading into their first-ever appearance on ABC's brand new Monday Night Football. Their opponents, the St Louis Cardinals, thoroughly humiliated them, 38-0, bringing the long, loud booing of Morton to ring through the Cotton Bowl.

The season is remembered as a strange one in Dallas. The quarterback question was unanswered, and the receivers were in turmoil. Bob Hayes had been benched briefly for poor performance, and Lance Rentzel was convicted on a morals charge. The Cowboys' four losses also included a 54-13 humiliation by the Minnesota Vikings. Coach Tom Landry had pushed his team to near greatness over the previous five seasons, twice taking them to the brink in the NFL championship game against the dynastic Green Bay Packers. In the hours after the devastating loss to the Cardinals, he decided that perhaps he'd been pushing too hard, that his players themselves were pushing too hard to win. So, for the first time in his career, Landry decided to loosen things up a bit. Into the Cowboys' normally stringent practices he worked a little volleyball and touch football. The players couldn't believe that Landry actually was *encouraging* relaxation. In response, they ripped off five straight wins, including a 52-10 demolition of Houston in the final regular season game, to finish 10-4.

Defensive leadership had helped rally the team, with much of that coming from linebacker Lee Roy Jordan and defensive back Herb Adderley, the Green Bay great who had been traded to Dallas. The team's momentum carried right on into the playoffs, where they tightened the screws on the Detroit Lions, 5-0, despite a 4-of-18 passing performance by Morton (whose passing problems could be related to shoulder surgery the previous winter). Fortunately, the Cowboys had Thomas in their offense. His 135 yards rushing provided Dallas' only real power against Detroit. Jethro Pugh and George Andrie sacked Lions quarterback Greg Landry for a safety and Mike Clark kicked a 26-yard field goal for the points.

The NFC championship match with John Brodie and the San Francisco 49ers showed a familiar pattern. Brodie threw for 262 yards, but also gave up two interceptions. Craig Morton, on the other hand, com-

pleted only seven of 22 attempts, but he kept the ball out of San Francisco mitts. The real offensive story for Dallas was again Duane Thomas, who rushed 27 times for 143 yards and a touchdown, as the Cowboys advanced to the Super Bowl in Miami's Orange Bowl, 17-10. The Colts, as well, had their difficulties to overcome, the primary one being a coaching change. Baltimore owner Carroll Rosenbloom became disenchanted with coach Don Shula after the Colts' loss to the Jets in Super Bowl III. In the aftermath, Shula moved on to the NFL's newest franchise, the Miami Dolphins.

The choice to replace Shula was tall, quiet Don McCafferty, a long-time Colts assistant, first under Weeb Ewbank, then under Shula. The change was not unwelcomed by the players. Where Shula was emotional and, at times, tempestuous in his approach to the game, McCafferty was more relaxed in dealing with his athletes. 'Don has a great knowledge of football,' veteran quarterback Johnny Unitas told reporters. 'He is a calm, collected individual. He doesn't shout and scream. He is able to look at football objectively without getting carried away emotionally.' Defensive end Bubba Smith put it a different way: '(McCafferty) treats you like a man, not like a dog.'

A bit of foreshadowing introduced the season for the Colts, as rookie placekicker Jim O'Brien kicked a last-second field goal to defeat the San Diego Chargers 16-14, in the opening game. The Baltimore defense – built on Smith, Mike Curtis, Ted Hendricks, Rick Volk and Jerry Logan – showed much promise. But the offense showed mostly age. Unitas, at 37, was beset with elbow tenderness. After 15 years of pro experience, he held all of the NFL's career passing records, and while his arm still held some zing, the smoke was mostly gone from his once-blazing sideline passes. Depending on their ailments, he and veteran Earl Morrall revolved in and out of the lineup.

The second game, a 44-24 loss to Kansas City, caused some tremors and shakeups in the offense. But from there, the Colts went on to post an 11-2-1 regular season record that included a 35-0 victory over Shula's Dolphins, then a 34-17 loss to the same team a few weeks later.

The playoffs brought a solid 17-0 whipping of the Cincinnati Bengals, then a showdown with the Oakland Raiders, who had won the West with an 8-4-2 record, mainly on the last-minute kicking and throwing of 43-year-old George Blanda subbing for the often injured Daryle Lamonica.

The old men, Blanda and Unitas, faced each other in the AFC championship game. Blanda completed 17 of 32 for 271 yards, but those figures included three key interceptions as the Raiders drove toward scores late in the game. Unitas completed only 11 of 30 attempts for 245 yards, but he clinched the victory with a 68-yard scoring pass to Ray Perkins. With the 27-17 victory, Baltimore had a date in Miami.

The only problem with the playoff outcome was that for the first time in the five-year history of the Super Bowl there was no 'AFL' team participating. Suddenly, the event had lost its basic chemistry, its David verses Goliath scenario. Just two years earlier,

Baltimore was representing the old guard NFL. Now, it was the AFC entry. Somehow that just didn't capture the fancy of the fans. The atmosphere may have sagged a bit, as numerous sports columnists about the country pointed out. But there was still plenty of controversy. Mainly, a group of fans in Florida had filed a lawsuit against the NFL's practice of blacking out games on local television even though the stadium seats were sold out for the game. NFL commissioner Pete Rozelle believed that allowing the games to be televised locally would eventually bring the erosion of stadium attendance. The Florida state courts ruled they had no jurisdiction in the case in the days before the Super Bowl, yet it would be only a matter of time before the NFL would have to drop its blackout policy for games that were already sold out.

To say the least, this was not a Super Bowl tailormade for hype. Dallas coach Tom Landry was stonefaced and reserved. McCafferty was laid back. Both teams had aging offenses and relied on their defenses for winning. The media tried to stir the coals in the well-known Unitas story.

'It's another game,' Unitas told reporters when asked about the importance of the Super Bowl. 'The money makes it different.' When they asked about his aging arm and his feelings when fans booed, Unitas said, 'I don't care. I can't care. I don't care what people say and I don't care what you write. All that matters is the team, the game and winning.'

For Baltimore, the main objective was to salve its wounds over the loss to the Jets in Super Bowl III. 'We felt we had as fine a football team as had ever been put together, and then you wake up and find that you're a bunch of bums,' Rosenbloom said of the loss. 'It's not the most pleasant thing in life. It's like finding your wife running around with another guy.' Rosenbloom had scheduled a victory party for his players after Super Bowl III. He still held the party, but the atmosphere was anything but victory. After Super Bowl V, the owner could finally hold a legitimate celebration, sort of. There was a definite sense after the game that there were no winners, just survivors.

The teams shared 11 turnovers between them. The Colts gave up three interceptions and four fumbles, and in the process, they shattered the myth that the team with the most turnovers loses. The Cowboys threw three interceptions and fumbled once, the big difference being that their one fumble robbed them of the opportunity to snuff the hope out of Baltimore hearts. In the third quarter, Dallas faced a first and goal at the Colt one when Thomas fumbled. If the Cowboys had scored, they would have led 20-6. 'If he'd scored,' Landry said, 'they would have had a lot of catching up to do. We would have been in firm control. But he fumbled because of his second effort on the play.'

Dallas got its big chance early when Baltimore's Ron Gardin fumbled a punt on his own nine. The Cowboys recovered, but missed on a touchdown when Morton overthrew receiver Reggie Rucker in the end zone. Mike Clark kicked a field goal for a 3-0 lead. In the second quarter, Dallas advanced to the Baltimore seven, but two more Morton passes failed, and Clark pushed the lead to 6-0 with his second field goal.

From there it was Baltimore's turn to bloop. Unitas threw a pass 20 yards deep and high to receiver Eddie Hinton. The ball passed through a Dallas defender's hands and on to Baltimore's John Mackey, who ran 45 yards for the touchdown. It went down in the books as a 75-yard TD pass. When Mark Washington blocked O'Brien's conversion attempt, the score was tied at 6. On the next Baltimore series, Unitas fumbled after being hit by Lee Roy Jordan. Dallas took over at the Colt 28, and moments later, Morton threw a seven-yard scoring pass to Thomas.

Further Baltimore problems developed on the next series when Unitas threw an interception and was injured on the play. He was replaced by Morrall and didn't return the rest of the day. On the next Baltimore series, Morrall calmly directed the Colts to the Dallas goal line, where three times Norm Bulaich bucked for the score and couldn't gain the end zone. On fourth down, McCafferty decided to go for it, but Morrall's pass fell incomplete. The decision not to kick the field goal grew heavier as the last two quarters developed. After Dallas got its own dash of anguish in the third quarter with Thomas' fumble, the Colts resumed their klutz act when Eddie Hinton fumbled just as a flea-flicker play appeared to break for a touchdown. The loose ball rolled out of the end zone and was ruled a touchback for the Cowboys, who despite all the turnovers still held to their 13-6 lead.

That changed a few plays later when a Morton pass was tipped by the Cowboys' Walt Garrison and intercepted by Rick Volk. Minutes later, Colt running back Tom Nowatzke scored on a dive to tie the game

Top left: *RB Tom Nowatzke led the Colts in rushing, but his 33 yards were only about half of Garrison's total.*

Bottom left: *Cowboy RB Duane Thomas rushed for 35 and made 21 more receiving.*

Right: *Morrall confers with Colts coach Don McCafferty.*

15
15
43
24

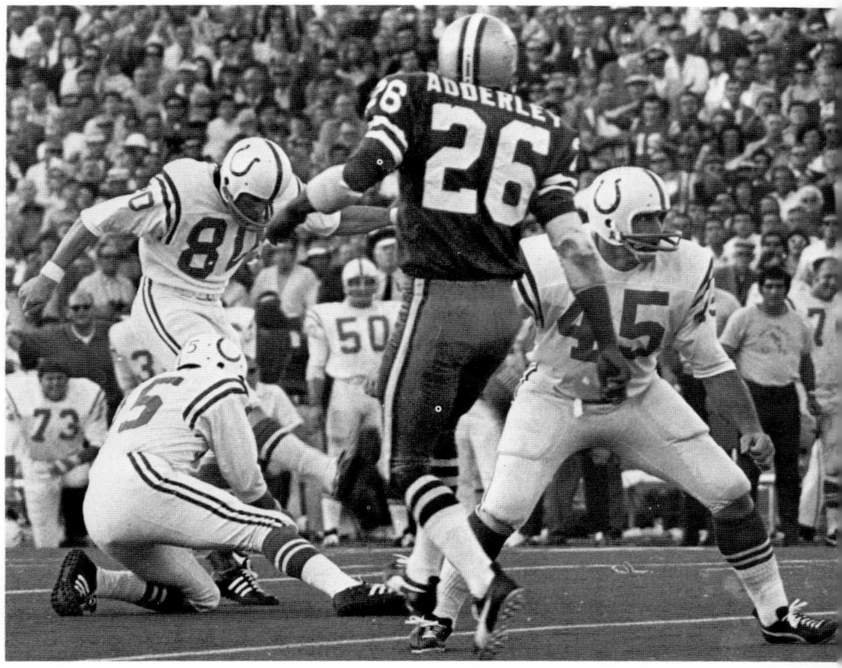

Far left: *With the score tied at 13 Colt Jim O'Brien's (80) field goal won the game in the last five seconds.*

Left: *Cowboy WR Reggie Rucker being bulldogged by the Colts.*

Above: *Another shot of the winning O'Brien kick. Morrall holds, RB Jerry Hill (45) is blocking and Cowboy cornerback Herb Adderley is too late to interfere. O'Brien had had a dream that an FG would win the game.*

at 13. Then, more than ever, McCafferty wished he had gone for the field goal earlier.

With less than two minutes left, the Cowboys started upfield one more time from their 27. A Morton pass, however, seemed to slip through Dan Reeves' hands and was intercepted by Mike Curtis. The Colts bled the clock down with a few plays, then allowed O'Brien to try the kick with five seconds left.

Arthur Dailey of the *New York Times* breathed a sigh of frustrated relief that it was over. For the two teams to go into overtime would have been only torture for the fans, he wrote, calling the game 'a sandlot exhibition between a couple of ball clubs of Lilliputian dimensions and miniscule skills.'

The rookie O'Brien, however, saw nothing flaky about the finish. 'Right after we got down here,' he told the crowd of reporters in the locker room, 'I had a dream that a long field goal was going to win this game. I didn't know who was going to kick or how far or when it would happen, but now I know. All the guys had confidence in me, that was the big thing. When we went out there, Earl Morrall, my holder, just told me to kick it straight through, that there was no wind – just to kick it.'

The rookie coach, was elated. 'The turning point of the game had to be Mike Curtis' interception,' he said. 'That set up the winning field goal for us. We had a lot of bad breaks in the first half but we hung in there. These guys are just fantastic.'

Asked what he had said to his players, Landry responded, 'You can't say anything. I tried, but I can't say anything after a game like this. We beat ourselves. The fumble and the two interceptions just killed us.'

Thomas left the locker room before reporters were allowed in. But Morton, who had fought back from shoulder surgery to face a season of struggle, answered questions for the post mortem. 'We just made too many mistakes,' he said. 'Their defenses didn't do anything we didn't expect. But they shut down our run, especially in the second half. And we've been a running team. I don't know what they did – maybe they changed up front.'

Reeves, the player-coach, summed it up: 'This was the biggest game we ever played. I just wish we could have won it. What hurts most was giving up 10 points on two tipped plays.'

In the survivors' locker room, Vince Lombardi's widow, Marie, presented Rosenbloom with the Lombardi Trophy. 'There is only one Vince Lombardi,' Rosenbloom said in his acceptance speech, 'and there'll never be another one like him.' No one doubted, or has ever doubted, that he was right.

Certainly, the game hadn't offered the kind of football precision Lombardi demanded, but the winners didn't mind. 'It may have looked sloppy,' said Colts safety Jerry Logan, 'but it was a great defensive football game.'

70
32

Super Bowl VI

Dallas Cowboys 24, Miami Dolphins 3

16 January 1972
Tulane Stadium, New Orleans
Attendance: 81,023

Dallas	3	7	7	7	—	24
Miami	0	3	0	0	—	3

Dallas – Field goal, 9, Clark.
Dallas – Alworth, 7, pass from Staubach (Clark kick).
Miami – Field goal, 31, Yepremian.
Dallas – D Thomas, 3, run (Clark kick).
Dallas – Ditka, 7, pass from Staubach (Clark kick).

Rushing: *Dallas* – D Thomas, 19 for 95, 1 TD; Garrison, 14 for 74; Hill, 7 for 25; Staubach, 5 for 18; Ditka, 1 for 17; Hayes, 1 for 16; Reeves, 1 for 7. *Miami* – Csonka, 9 for 40; Kiick, 10 for 40; Griese, 1 for 0.
Passing: *Dallas* – Staubach, 12 of 19 for 119, 2 TD. *Miami* – Griese, 12 of 23 for 134, 1 int.
Receiving: *Dallas* – D Thomas, 3 for 17; Alworth, 2 for 28, 1 TD; Ditka, 2 for 28, 1 TD; Hayes, 2 for 23; Garrison, 2 for 11; Hill, 1 for 12. *Miami* – Warfield, 4 for 39; Kiick, 3 for 21; Csonka, 2 for 18; Fleming, 1 for 27; Twilley, 1 for 20; Mandich, 1 for 9.
Punting: *Dallas* – Widby, 5 for 37.2 average. *Miami* – Seiple, 5 for 40.0.
Punt Returns: *Dallas* – Hayes, 1 for –1. *Miami* – Scott, 1 for 21.
Kickoff Returns: *Dallas* – I Thomas, 1 for 23; Waters, 1 for 11, *Miami* – Morris, 4 for 90; Ginn, 1 for 32.
Interceptions: *Dallas* – Howley, 1 for 41. *Miami* – None.

Super Bowl VI. The Cowboys' Walt Garrison carries. No 12 is QB Roger Staubach, and No 70 is tackle Rayfield Wright.

In March of 1971, the 26 executives of the NFL gathered in Palm Beach, Florida to decide the site of Super Bowl VI. They quickly became deadlocked at 13-13 over whether to play the game in Dallas or Miami. The main objection was that both the Dolphins and the Cowboys had strong teams, and no one wanted one of the two to have a distinct home-field advantage. So the group finally compromised and sent the game to Tulane Stadium in New Orleans, which needed a bit of paint here and there but offered 81,000 seats to hold the Super crowd.

The decision, as the season soon showed, was a good one. Both Dallas and Miami played their way to the Super Bowl, giving the game what you might call a new round of old faces. There were Don Shula and Earl Morrall, only this time they were Dolphins instead of Colts. And, of course, there was Tom Landry with his Cowpokes. But the most veteran of all Super Bowlers was Dallas defensive back and future Hall of Famer, Herb Adderley, who was making his fourth appearance in the games, twice as a Green Bay star, twice as a Dallas defensive stalwart. His earnings for playing in those four games would come to the unheard-of sum in 1971 of $106,000. But for the Cowboys, the matter really wasn't the money, it was the championship. They had narrowly lost the NFL title to Green Bay in 1966 and 1967. The Cleveland Browns beat them in the '69 playoffs. Then Baltimore had outlasted them in Super Bowl V.

At first, the 1971 season developed poorly for Dallas, with Landry alternating Craig Morton and Roger Staubach at quarterback. Also Duane Thomas sat out the first few games in a salary dispute. After the first seven games, the Cowboys stood 4-3. Then Landry made Staubach his starter, and Dallas didn't lose another one the rest of the season. Morton, a solid deep pocket passer, and Staubach, a roll-out quarterback, both offered good throwing arms, but Staubach had the added dimension of his running ability. And as time would reveal, he had an uncanny knack for the two-minute drill and the comeback. In 1971, however, he was relatively inexperienced, having served four years in the navy, including a stint in Vietnam, after winning the Heisman Trophy in 1962 for the US Naval Academy.

Landry still called all of Staubach's plays from the sideline, and the coach worried about his quarterback's penchant for breaking out of the passing pocket and running. But the team's needs and Staubach's considerable talents had combined to force the change. 'Roger runs when he cannot find open receivers,' Landry said succinctly. 'But I wish he would not.'

Staubach was frank in his appraisal: 'Naturally I want to call the plays, to be the complete quarterback. But I'm not ready yet.'

'Maybe next year,' Landry said.

Over the season, Staubach would rush for 343 yards, averaging 8.1 yards per attempt. He also completed 126 of 211 passing attempts for 1882 yards and 15 touchdowns against only four interceptions, the numbers of a genuine all-pro performance.

Far left: *Miami QB Bob Griese takes the snap.*

Above: *Dolphin Nick Buoniconti (85) closes on Duane Thomas.*

Left: *Miami WR Paul Warfield.*

Against the Minnesota Vikings in the first round of the playoffs, Staubach ruled the defensive struggle with proficiency. He completed 10 of 14 passes for 99 yards and a touchdown as Dallas won, 20-12.

In the other divisional playoff game, John Brodie and the San Francisco 49ers had ousted the Washington Redskins, 24-20. The 49ers came to Texas Stadium for the NFC championship game, where Staubach rushed for 55 yards and passed for another 103 as the Cowboys advanced to their second straight Super Bowl, 14-3. In the AFC, Shula had engineered a remarkable turnaround for the Dolphins after arriving in Miami in 1970. He had taken over a three-win team that first year and drove them to the

playoffs. For 1971, Shula and his troops tiptoed to the Eastern Division title with a 10-3-1 record. In shifting from Baltimore to Miami, Shula apparently took the edge from his temper and softened his emotional approach to the game. That seemed to suit his talented offense just fine.

The Miami running game moved on the wheels of fullback Larry Csonka, who had rushed for 1051 yards over the season, and Jim Kiick, who had 738 yards. Their fans dubbed the Miami backfield 'Butch Cassidy and The Sundance Kid.' Quarterback Bob Griese, a former Purdue All-American, and receiver Paul Warfield gave the Dolphins a passing game. For 1971, Griese completed 55 percent of his passes for 2089 yards and 19 touchdowns against nine interceptions. Warfield had caught 43 passes for a whopping 996 yards, an average of 24 yards per catch. He had scored 11 touchdowns.

'Bob has a magnificent football brain,' Shula said of Griese. 'He is second to none in the huddle or at the line of scrimmage.' For Griese, the challenge of quarterbacking was a matter of maintaining one's cool in the midst of chaos. 'You never allow yourself to panic,' he said. 'You can't quarterback a team with the idea that you're going to score 20 points in one march. It's seven at a time at the best. You must stick with the game plan.'

Warfield, a future Hall of Famer, had come into the NFL in 1964 as a first-round draft pick of the Cleveland Browns. 'I had been a running back and a defensive back at Ohio State,' he said, 'but when I arrived at the Browns' training camp, they had Ray Renfro there to teach me. He had been a great wide receiver. He'd describe the pattern, demonstrate it and then I'd run it. And as I was taught by Renfro, the effectiveness of a receiver on a defensive back depends on how well he is able to close the gap between him and the defender. . . . Because at that instant when I'm closest to him, it's a moment of truth for him. He has to make a decision on me. If I'm that close to him, the defender is afraid of getting beat deep, but if I make my cut too soon, three or four yards away from him, then he'll have time to recover.'

Once in the playoffs, the Dolphins' path to Super Bowl VI was arduous. It included the longest game in pro football history – the Christmas Day 1971 AFC playoff with the Kansas City Chiefs. The game was a kicking duel pitting Miami's Garo Yepremian against Kansas City's Jan Stenerud. It also featured the All Star performance of the Chiefs' Ed Podolak, the fearsome play of Kansas City linebacker Willie Lanier, the passing of Len Dawson and Griese, and the inside/outside of Kiick and Csonka. After six periods of play, two sudden-death overtimes, 82 minutes, 40 seconds of action, the game came down to a photo finish. The Dolphins had never beaten Kansas City in the previous six games the two teams had played. Both had finished with 10-3-1 records, but it appeared that Kansas City was headed for a seventh straight victory when the Chiefs scored 10 quick points. The Dolphins scored the same number in the second quarter, and the second half became a touchdown barter session, with each team trading two.

The memorable performance came from Podolak, who totalled 350 all purpose yards – 100 rushing, 100 receiving and 150 returning kicks. But in the end, the

Far left: *Defensive end Pat Toomay of Dallas' 'Doomsday Defense' looms over hapless Dolphin QB Bob Griese.*

Left: *Miami's first score was on a 31-yard field goal by Garo Yepremian.*

Right: *Before the AFC playoff game between Kansas City and Miami the Chiefs' Jan Stenerud had been picked to represent the AFC in the Pro Bowl, an undeserved slight to Yepremian.*

game was decided by placekickers. The night before the game, Stenerud was named to represent the AFC in the Pro Bowl, a slight to Yepremian, who had led the conference in scoring. Stenerud had a chance to win the game with seconds left in regulation, but missed from the 31-yard line. He got a second try in the first overtime, from 42 yards out, but Miami linebacker Nick Buoniconti broke through the line and snuffed it.

When Yepremian missed from 52 yards, the game slipped into its second overtime. Weariness became the primary factor, but Csonka drew on his reserves for a 29-yard run to set up Yepremian for another 37-yard try. He calmly kicked the game winner, as Miami advanced, 27-24.

In the AFC championship game against the Baltimore Colts, Griese opened the scoring by connecting with Warfield on a 75-yard touchdown pass. The defense later intercepted a John Unitas pass and ran it back for a touchdown and Csonka scored on a 12-yard run to give the Dolphins a 21-0 win.

In the early morning hours the next day, Shula was watching a game film when the phone rang. The late caller was President Richard Nixon, who wanted to suggest that the Miami coach make use of a 'down and in' play for Warfield against the Cowboys in the Super Bowl. The press got word of the phone call and made much about it in the days before the game. Reporters also played off the fact that Tom Landry was a friend of evangelist Billy Graham, who in turn was a friend of Nixon's. Reporters asked Landry if he wanted Graham to suggest a play for the Cowboys. 'I'd rather take Billy's prayers,' Landry said of Graham's help. 'I know they will be better than any play he has.'

Asked about the President's play, Warfield said, 'On the Dolphins, we have about seven basic patterns – the square-out, the square-in, the hook or curl, the slant-in, the takeoff, the post, the Z and the deep. But each man has at least one variation. The total would be around 20 different patterns. We don't have a down-and-in in our nomenclature. But it would be a slant-in if it were about 10 to 15 yards deep and a post if about 30 yards deep.'

Whatever the play was called, the Cowboys were ready for it. 'They had two weeks to prepare,' Warfield said after the game. 'And they made sure that under any circumstance we wouldn't be able to complete that pass.'

On the other hand, the Dallas offense worked with spare precision, driving to a score in each quarter. The Cowboys opened with a Mike Clark field goal.

Then with 75 seconds left in the first half, Staubach threw seven yards to Lance Alworth for a 10-0 lead. Alworth was jammed in the corner, but Staubach delivered the ball with a zip chest high. Alworth grabbed it quickly and stepped into the end zone. Mike Clark kicked the extra point.

The Dolphins rushed back downfield and with four seconds left Yepremian kicked a 31-yard field goal. But they continued to struggle in the second half as Dallas put the game out of reach. Duane Thomas scored on a three-yard run in the third, and Staubach threw another TD pass in the fourth, this time to tight end Mike Ditka for an insurmountable 24-3 lead.

The story was Dallas' record-setting, ball-control ground game. Thomas rushed 19 times for 95 yards. Walt Garrison went 14 for 74 and Calvin Hill added another 25 as the Cowpokes set a Super Bowl record of 252 yards on the ground. The legendary Red Smith viewed the game and, ever ready with a memorable phrase, commented that the Dallas backs 'operated like infuriated beer trucks.'

On the day, Staubach completed 12 of 19 attempts for 119 yards and two touchdowns. He was selected the game's Most Valuable Player by *Sport* magazine. The key Miami statistics were turnovers: two fumbles and an interception.

Dallas officials basked in the glow of the moment. 'This is the successful conclusion of our 12-year plan,' owner Clint Murchison said of the team's perseverance with coach Tom Landry through the franchise's first dozen years.

'I can't describe how we feel,' Landry said. 'We fought so hard, came so close so many times. It's great for players like Bob Lilly and Chuck Howley who have been with the team for so long.' Both players had come to the Cowboys in 1961 and endured the lean seasons as Landry built the franchise. Lilly smiled broadly and told reporters: 'I feel like I lost two years off my age. I feel 29 again.'

'We were all so determined, no one could stop us,' Landry said. 'We ran extremely well.'

As for Thomas, he dressed quietly amid the din and later conferred with his adviser, Jim Brown. When Thomas turned aside reporters' questions, Brown said, 'Duane's his own man. He's one of the greatest backs who ever lived. He should get more money.'

The Dolphins, meanwhile, were left to rebuild their dream. Shula had become the first coach to lose two Super Bowls. 'I'm very disappointed,' he said. 'The Cowboys tore us apart defensively. They made one mistake, a fumble, but that came when the game was already over. The only way we can make up for it is to win the Super Bowl another time. Winning 'x' number of games won't make up for this.'

His words would prove prophetic for the '72 season. Warfield projected an optimism beyond Shula's determination. 'We're capable of coming back next year and being in this game,' the receiver said, 'because we've been here and we have a good young club.'

Well and good, but the question was, could they win it?

Left: *Garrison carries on a handoff from Staubach.*

Left below: *Duane Thomas makes Dallas' second TD.*

Above: *Dallas coach Tom Landry.*

Below: Cowboy defensemen Bob Lilly (74), Jethro Pugh (75) and Larry Cole (63).

Super Bowl VII

Miami Dolphins 14, Washington Redskins 7

14 January 1973
Los Angeles Memorial Coliseum
Attendance: 90,182

Miami	7	7	0	0	—	14
WAshington	0	0	0	7	—	7

Miami – Twilley, 28, pass from Griese (Yepremian kick).
Miami – Kiick, 1, run (Yepremian kick).
Washington – Bass, 49, fumble return (Knight kick).

Rushing: *Miami* – Csonka, 15 for 112; Kiick, 12 for 38, 1 TD; Morris, 10 for 34. *Washington* – Brown, 22 for 72; Harraway, 10 for 37; Kilmer, 2 for 18; C Taylor, 1 for 8; Smith, 1 for 6.
Passing: *Miami* – Griese, 8 of 11 for 88, 1 TD, 1 int. *Washington* – Kilmer, 14 of 28 for 104, 3 int.
Receiving: *Miami* – Warfield, 3 for 36; Kiick, 2 for 6; Twilley, 1 for 28, 1 TD; Mandich, 1 for 19, Csonka, 1 for –1. *Washington* – Jefferson, 5 for 50; Brown, 5 for 26; C Taylor, 2 for 20; Smith, 1 for 11; Harraway, 1 for –3.
Punting: *Miami* – Seiple, 7 for 43.0 average. *Washington* – Bragg, 5 for 31.2.
Punt Returns: *Miami* – Scott, 2 for 4. *Washington* – Haymond, 4 for 9.
Kickoff Returns: *Miami* – Morris, 2 for 33. *Washington* – Haymond, 2 for 30; Mul-Key, 1 for 15.
Interceptions: *Miami* – Scott, 2 for 63; Buoniconti, 1 for 32. *Washington* – Owens, 1 for 0.

Super Bowl VII. Redskin RB Larry Brown runs into a solid wall of Miami's 'No Name' defenders.

In the 53-year history of the National Football League, no team had ever achieved a perfect, unbeaten, untied season. Over the years, it always seemed that something – a missed block, a fumbled snap, a blocked punt – tripped up the teams of destiny. The Canton Bulldogs finished unbeaten in both 1923 and 1924, but ties spotted their records. The same was true of the 1929 Green Bay Packers, who ripped through 12 wins and a tie.

The Chicago Bears had come closest in 1934, when they ran to a 13-0 regular season record and were leading 13-3 against the New York Giants heading into the fourth quarter of the NFL championship game in frozen weather at New York's Polo Grounds. But in a famous reversal, the Giants donned tennis shoes at halftime and turned the fourth quarter into a track meet, blasting Chicago's perfect season hopes, 30-13. The Bears got close again in 1942, battering to an 11-0 regular season record only to lose, 14-7, to the Washington Redskins in the NFL title game.

But the idea of a perfect season dimmed considerably after those early years. The competition had become too balanced, the schedule too long for a team to go undefeated, observers thought. That thinking changed, of course, with the arrival of the Don Shula's 1972 Miami Dolphins.

With his team's loss in Super Bowl VI, Don Shula had become the first coach to lose two Super Bowls. Going into the next season, he had a demon to exorcise. He had been the coach of the heavily favored Baltimore Colts when they were trimmed by Joe Namath and the New York Jets in 1969. The outcome had left difficult feelings between Shula and Colts owner Carroll Rosenbloom. So in 1970, Shula moved to the Miami Dolphins' struggling young franchise. While the Dolphins' quick rise confirmed his coaching genius, their Super Bowl loss to the Cowboys brought back a flood of doubt.

The Dolphins began training camp that next summer with a whirlwind of intensity. The high pressure system creating it was Shula's considerable pride. ('He hates to lose,' Shula's mother, Mary, said of her son. 'When he was eight years old, he would play cards with his grandmother. If he lost, he would tear up the cards and run and hide under the porch. You couldn't pry him out for supper.') He wanted nothing less than absolute victory. And he had a team that could give it to him. In three years, Shula had built the perfect pro football machine, and he had done so with proven football formulas: conservative, run-oriented offense, a strong kicking game and rock-ribbed defense.

Running backs Larry Csonka, Mercury Morris and Jim Kiick powered the Dolphins' considerable ground game. They would have a nonpareil season with Csonka gaining 1117 yards and Morris 1000, making them the first teammates in league history to rush for 1000 yards each in the same season. The four interior linemen whose blocking helped get them there – Norm Evans, Bob Keuchenberg, Larry Little and Jim Langer – had all been turned loose by other pro teams.

The air game, of course, hinged on Bob Griese throwing to a corps of receivers, with Paul Warfield and Howard Twilley getting the most work. Placekicker Garo Yepremian made 24 of 37 field goal attempts over the season. That and the ground game's steady production made the Dolphins the highest scoring team in the NFL with 385 points over 14 games.

Top: *The game's great issue was: Would Don Shula's Miami team have the first perfect season in NFL history?*

Above: *Miami QB Bob Griese.*

Right: *Dolphin FB Larry Csonka follows his interference as Redskin linebacker Jack Pardee circles behind.*

For all the flash and dash of the offense, the Dolphins' real strength was their defense, that infamous group inadvertantly named by Tom Landry before Super Bowl VI when he told reporters, 'I can't recall the names of the Miami defensive unit, but they're of big concern to me.' Thus, it became the 'No-Name Defense,' a moniker the media applied with their own special sort of glue. It stuck and dried quickly in the hot air of Super Bowl VI and in the process became an item of pride to the unit's members. Later, Miami fans attempted to hold a contest to find a more distinguished name, but the defenders would have none of it. They liked their no-name just the way it was.

The names among the no-name crowd were line-

backer Nick Buoniconti, defensive back Jake Scott and tackle Manny Fernandez. In 1972 they would play as few defenses have, giving up a league-low 186 points over the 14 regular season games. The architect of this stinginess was Bill Arnsparger, Shula's defensive coach since 1964. 'Good defensive football,' Arnsparger offered as his precept, 'means having your people converge around the ball as if they were a swarm of bees.' Beyond the swarm mentality, Arnsparger brought complete organization and planning to the Dolphins' defense. 'Some coaches pull the defenses out of a hat,' Buoniconti told reporters, 'but not him. There's never any guesswork on my part regarding what coverage to use, or what blitz to use, or what situation to use them in. During a game, he never gets flustered, he never lets the pressure affect him. Even during the Super Bowl last year, Arnsparger didn't get excited. He just kept telling us we had to tackle better.'

The Miami talent gathered as a storm on opening day and started with a fury, levelling Kansas City and Houston before reaching a brief lull against Minnesota. After a narrow 16-14 win over the Vikings, the Dolphins blew past the New York Jets and San Diego, then paused to struggle with Buffalo. Again, Shula's intensity was the driving force behind a 24-23 victory. Three games, three victories later, Griese broke an ankle and had to be replaced by 38-year-old Earl Morrall. (In a moment of premonition, Shula had acquired Morrall from the New York Giants in the offseason for only $100.) The storm seemed to have dissipated to a squall, but with Morrall leading, Miami regained its pace, slicing through nine straight opponents to finish the regular season, 14-0.

The first round of the playoffs brought a low point, as the Cleveland Browns played tough, until Miami finally subdued them, 20-14. The special teams played a big role in the win, as Charlie Babb returned a blocked punt for a touchdown in the first half. Yepremian also kicked two field goals.

Terry Bradshaw and the Pittsburgh Steelers had

reached their first AFC championship game on the strength of Franco Harris' 'immaculate reception' in the opening round playoffs against the Oakland Raiders. The Steelers took a 7-0 lead early against Miami and appeared ready to end their season with another first-half drive. But Bradshaw was knocked dizzy and fumbled at the Miami three. Dolphin punter Larry Seiple ran 37 yards for a first down in the second quarter that kept a drive alive and allowed Miami to tie the score at 7.

The second half brought more battling and the appearance of Griese in relief of Morrall. Griese connected with Warfield for a 52-yard pass play, and moments later Miami took a 14-10 lead on Kiick's two-yard dive. After Kiick scored again to stretch the lead to 21-10; Bradshaw returned for Pittsburgh and tightened the game to 21-17 with a touchdown pass. The momentum appeared to shift to the Steelers, but their last two drives ended when Bradshaw threw interceptions. The Dolphins extended their record to 16-0, but more important, they were headed to the Super Bowl against the NFC champions, the Washington Redskins.

As with Miami, Washington also relied on the ground game. The tomahawk in the Redskin armory was Larry Brown, who had rushed for 1286 yards in 285 carries. If opponents played the run too closely, quarterback Billy Kilmer threw his floating butterball passes to receivers Charley Taylor, Jerry Smith

Top left: *Washington QB Billy Kilmer (17) hands off to Larry Brown (43).*

Bottom left: *Kilmer takes aim.*

Above: *Redskin wide receiver Charley Taylor had only a fair day, catching two for 20 and rushing eight. Taylor had been with Washington since 1964.*

and Roy Jefferson. They were the 'Over The Hill Gang,' named for coach George Allen's strategy of trading future draft picks for experienced but aging talent. There were those who openly accused Allen of throwing away the club's future for his own short-term goals. 'The future is now,' was his simple response to his critics.

Allen was another in a line of intense, workaholic coaches who had fought and scratched their way to the Super Bowl. Perhaps Allen's distinction was that he was even more intense, more of a workaholic than the rest. Sportswriters looking of evidence for that found documentation from his wife, Etty, who talked about Allen's late-night trading and bartering of players. 'He's in bed next to me, and I hear him on the phone at three am making those calls to the West Coast,' she confided.

He was the type of coach who would lead Redskin cheers in the locker room and somehow get his veteran players to join in. ('Can you imagine me leading Larry Csonka in singing 'Three Cheers For the Dolphins'?' Shula asked reporters.) Allen was not liked around the league. Earlier in his career he had broken a contract with the Chicago Bears to take a coaching job with the Los Angeles Rams, prompting George Halas to file a suit against him. Halas brought the case to court and won, then dropped the matter satisfied he had proved his point. Halas called Allen an opportunist, a liar, a schemer, a cheat, a man without character. Vince Lombardi listened to the tirade, then turned to Rams owner Dan Reeves and reportedly said, 'Damn, sounds as if you're getting a helluva football coach.'

Although Allen won regularly with the Rams, Reeves later accused him of spending and lying extravagantly. Redskins owner Edward Bennett Williams gave Allen a $125,000 salary and the authority to spend money for talent. 'George Allen was given an unlimited expense account and he has already exceeded it,' Williams quipped. President Richard Nixon was an intense Washington fan and a friend of Allen's. The President frequently phoned the coach for strategy discussions.

Allen's mindset was defensive. He was totally absorbed by the subject and collected the talent to master the challenge. With Verlon Biggs at defensive end, Bill Brundige and Diron Talbert at tackle, Jack Pardee, Chris Hanburger and Harold McClinton at linebacker, and Mike Bass and Pat Fischer in the secondary, Allen produced the NFC's toughest defense. He cared very little for offense and left those matters to his coordinator, Ted Marchibroda. 'George leaves me alone,' Marchibroda told reporters. 'He doesn't even approve the game plan. He's concerned with the defense.'

With that modus operandi, Washington zipped through the regular season with an 11-3 record, then added playoff victories over Green Bay and Dallas for the right to meet Miami at the Los Angeles Memorial Coliseum. The 26-3 victory over Roger Staubach and Dallas in the NFC title game was particularly satisfying. The Redskins had finally unseated the Cowboys from their perch atop the conference. Kilmer had turned in a near-perfect day, completing 14 of 18 passing attempts for 194 yards and two touchdowns. Curt Knight kicked four field goals.

The Dolphins had rolled over their regular season opponents. But that mattered little to Shula. A loss in the Super Bowl would only make them losers again. He wanted nothing short of complete victory. As if the silent anxiety weren't enough, Rosenbloom, who had acquired ownership of the Los Angeles Rams, commented to the press that Shula would choke again in the big game. If Shula felt the pressure, he

didn't show it. In the press conferences he was all smiles and confidence. 'I'm 0-2 in Super Bowls,' he told reporters. 'I intend to be 1-2 after Sunday.'

Griese had come back from his injury to guide the team to a late touchdown for the win over Pittsburgh, and Shula tabbed him as the starter in the Super Bowl, a decision made much of by the media. Morrall was the diplomat, saying that he preferred to start but understood Shula's decision.

The game, played before 90,000 at Memorial Coliseum in Los Angeles, was controlled by Miami's efficiency. After an early exchange of possessions, the No-Name Defense pinned the Redskins in their own territory. Miami scored in each of the first two quarters, and settled in to dominate the second half defensively. The Redskins' threat was almost nonexistent until just under two minutes to play, when the Skins blocked a 42-yard field goal by Yepremian. The kicker retrieved the loose ball and weakly attempted to pass. Washington's Mike Bass intercepted the ball and returned it 49 yards for a touchdown. With that momentum, Washington got the ball back with just under a minute left. But Jake Scott killed their last drive with his second interception of the day, and Shula finally had his Super Bowl trophy. Scott was later named the game's MVP by *Sport* magazine. Miami's star on offense was Csonka, who rushed for 112 yards on 15 carries. As expected, Shula was ecstatic afterwards in the locker room; he certainly had every right to be.

Shula's joy was matched only by Allen's disappointment. 'It doesn't do any good to play in the Super Bowl if you don't win,' he told reporters. 'We just lost to a team that played a better game . . . I can't get out of here fast enough. There will be a lot of hours of agony tonight.'

Nixon wired his condolences to Allen and his congratulations to Shula: 'Today's victory was a smashing climax to a perfect season,' the President told the Miami coach. As Shula was presented with the Lombardi Trophy, he confessed, 'All along, I've had an empty feeling. And this right here is the ultimate.'

As had been the practice since the Super Bowl began, the winners took home $15,000 each, the losing players $7500.

'With a 17-0 record, I don't know what we can do next year for an encore,' Shula said. 'But right now I'm just going to sit back and relish this for a while.'

Left top: *Coach George Allen had come to Washington in 1971 and had staffed his team with tough veterans.*

Left below: *Redskin RB Larry Brown (43) led his team in rushing with 72, but Csonka led the game with 112.*

Above left: *Dolphin QB Bob Griese (12) passed for 88 in the game, but the Redskins' Kilmer hit 104.*

Above right: *Dolphin RB Larry Csonka carries as guard Larry Little helps him out with some blocking.*

58
22
88

Super Bowl VIII

Miami Dolphins 24, Minnesota Vikings 7

13 January 1974
Rice Stadium, Houston
Attendance: 68,142

Minnesota	0	0	0	7	—	7
Miami	14	3	7	0	—	24

Miami – Csonka, 5, run (Yepremian kick).
Miami – Kiick, 1, run (Yepremian kick).
Miami – Field goal, 28, Yepremian.
Miami – Csonka, 2, run (Yepremian kick).
Minnesota – Tarkenton, 4, run (Cox kick).

Rushing: *Minnesota* – Reed, 11 for 32; Foreman, 7 for 18; Tarkenton, 4 for 17, 1 TD; Marinaro, 1 for 3; B Brown, 1 for 2. *Miami* – Csonka, 33 for 145, 2 TD; Morris, 11 for 34; Kiick, 7 for 10, 1 TD; Griese, 2 for 7.
Passing: *Minnesota* – Tarkenton, 18 of 28 for 182, 1 int. *Miami* – Griese, 6 of 7 for 73.
Receiving: *Minnesota* – Foreman, 5 for 27; Gilliam, 4 for 44; Voigt, 3 for 46; Marinaro, 2 for 39; B Brown, 1 for 9; Kingsriter, 1 for 9; Lash, 1 for 9; Reed, 1 for –1. *Miami* – Warfield, 2 for 33; Mandich, 2 for 21; Briscoe, 2 for 19.
Punting: *Minnesota* – Eischeid, 5 for 42.2 average. *Miami* – Seiple, 3 for 39.7.
Punt Returns: *Minnesota* – Bryant, 0 for 0. *Miami* – Scott, 3 for 20.
Kickoff Returns: *Minnesota* – Gilliam, 2 for 41; West, 2 for 28. *Miami* – Scott, 2 for 47.
Interceptions: *Minnesota* – None. *Miami* – Johnson, 1 for 10.

Super Bowl VIII. Dolphin RB Eugene 'Mercury' Morris tries to elude the grasp of Viking DT Alan Page (88).

Don Shula's Miami Dolphins stretched their incredible win string one game into the 1973 season, then tasted defeat for the first time in many months with a 12-7 loss to the Oakland Raiders. But from there, the Dolphins resumed their championship pace, dropping one more meaningless late-season game in the process, before offering one of the finest displays ever of pure football power on their way to a second consecutive Super Bowl title.

In the statistical category, the team was just a hair off from the previous year, when fullback Larry Csonka and running back Mercury Morris had become the first teammates in the history of football to gain 1000 yards rushing in a season. In 1973 Csonka rushed for 1003 yards and Morris for 954. And the team finished the regular season at 12-2. Yet, when the championship game had ended in Houston in January 1974, there was little doubt that Miami was one of pro football's all-time dominant teams, in a class with that other two-time Super Bowl winner, the 1966-67 Green Bay Packers.

There was some debate as to which team was greater. But Marv Fleming, who played on both Shula's and Lombardi's teams, had little doubt. 'This is the greatest team ever,' he said of the Dolphins. Team after team came to similar conclusions over the course of the season. Cincinnati, the first-round victim in the playoffs, watched as Morris dashed to the outside for 106 yards and Csonka pounded them inside for 79. Quarterback Bob Griese delivered the death blows, however, by throwing for 159 yards and two touchdowns, as Miami collected the thirteenth win of the year, 34-16.

The Oakland Raiders, meanwhile, had moved young Ken Stabler in at quarterback to replace a struggling Daryle Lamonica and seemed a solid challenger for the AFC title. Stabler had been deadly in the first round of the playoffs, completing 14 of 17 passes, as Oakland blasted Pittsburgh, 33-14. The Raiders hopes were high for Miami in the AFC championship game. But the Dolphins ground them under with their running attack. Csonka rushed for 117 yards, Morris for 86, and the Miami defense did the rest for a 27-10 blowout. For the third straight year, Shula's team was bound for the Super Bowl.

The Minnesota Vikings were the team to emerge from the NFC. With quarterback Fran Tarkenton, receiver John Gilliam and rookie running back Chuck Foreman, the Vikings ran to a 12-2 regular season record, including nine straight victories to open the schedule. When they were good, they were pretty good. But when they were bad, they were very bad, as evidenced by a late-season 27-0 blowout at the hands of the Cincinnati Bengals. But in the playoffs, Minnesota stabilized with a close win over the wildcard Washington Redskins.

Then in the NFC title game, the Vikings returned to their ball-control, power game and did in Dallas, 27-10. Minnesota's defense gave the team its real teeth, particularly the secondary, which picked off four Roger Staubach passes. In the second half, Bobby Bryant returned an interception 63 yards for the score that put the game out of the Cowboys' reach.

Above: *Ace QB Ken Stabler of the Oakland Raiders.*

Left: *In 1974 coach Don Shula brought the Dolphins to the Super Bowl for a record third straight time.*

Right: *Miami's Larry Csonka (barely visible in this big pile-up) carried for two TDs.*

The Dallas ground game was hampered by the absence of injured running back Calvin Hill and gained only 80 yards against the Vikings' veteran front four – 'The Purple People Eaters' – tackles Alan Page and Gary Larsen and ends Jim Marshall and Carl Eller. The NFC championship game was a display of power, but sportswriters immediately doubted that Minnesota would have the same kind of success against the Dolphins. If nothing else, observers agreed that Super Bowl VIII would be won or lost in the trenches.

Perhaps the only question for the Dolphins was whether their '53 defense' could be effective against the Minnesota ground game. The '53' was named for

EVANS
60
77
KIICK

linebacker/end Bob Matheson (No 53), who replaced a down lineman in many key situations. The '53' combined with Miami's zone pass coverage to give the Dolphins a variety of defensive options.

'What we're trying to do,' Miami defensive coach Bill Arnsparger said of the Matheson defense, 'is present the offense with a number of possibilities that complicates their execution. The more time they have to take to figure out what we're doing, the better chance we have of stopping them.' Matheson, Arnsparger explained to reporters, 'can come in at either linebacker or end, and it gives us a lot of versatility as to what we can do defensively.'

Shula focused on the offense, but had every bit of confidence in Arnsparger's defense. 'We can make the 53 hold up against the run,' Shula said in a press conference. 'We found that out in the playoffs against Cincinnati. We don't have any qualms about using the 53 in any situation.'

Houston had been selected as the site for the game because of its 18,000 first-class hotel rooms and Rice Stadium with 71,000 plus seats. To warm up the atmosphere, Commissioner Pete Rozelle and his wife Carolyn hosted a Texas hoedown in the Astrodome the day before the game, with 2836 guests, many of them sportswriters and team executives, chowing down on barbecue and Mexican food and listening to country music star Charlie Pride. 'There are more people at this party than we used to have at our games,' commented New England Patriots President Billy Sullivan as he surveyed the crowd.

The growth had been substantial in most other areas of the event, especially television, where a minute of prime advertising ran $212,000. CBS was handling the TV broadcasting of Super Bowl VIII and estimated its audience would shoot above 80 million (NBC had estimated the audience for Super Bowl VII at about 57 million). In all, the game would be viewed over 507 stations, 212 of them in the US. The network planned to use 15 cameras to televise the game and hired former Green Bay quarterback Bart Starr as a consultant in the control truck to help select action shots. Much of the pre-game talk centered on Tarkenton and the fact that he had finally become a winner after 13 years in the league. Other speculation focused on Paul Warfield's thigh injury and questions about his availability for the game.

After the game, a reporter asked Alan Page when

Far left: *Viking CB Charlie West returned two punts for 28.*

Left: *Viking Fran Tarkenton outpassed Griese 182 to 73.*

Above: *Miami's Larry Csonka set a Super Bowl record with 33 carries that produced a total of 145 yards rushing, a record that would last only a year.*

he knew Minnesota was in trouble. 'After the first few plays,' he replied. Stated simply, Shula used his power game, and Larry Csonka rushed for 145 yards as the Dolphins bulled to a 24-0 third-quarter lead, and coasted to the win, 24-7.

Miami opened the first quarter with a 62-yard, 10-play drive capped by Csonka's five-yard TD run. Then before the quarter ended, the Dolphins struck again, also another 10-play drive, with Jim Kiick doing the damage on a one-yard dive.

The Miami defense never allowed the Minnesota running attack room to get started. As a result, Tarkenton was forced to throw more, which he did reasonably well, completing 18 or 28 attempts for 182 yards. But the Dolphins' zone coverage and the lack of a ground game prevented the Vikings from sustaining a drive. Their one complete effort of the first half penetrated inside the Miami 20, but Dolphin safety Jake Scott recovered a fumble by Minnesota's Oscar Reed to snuff the uprising.

'It was very helpful to us to get ahead,' Arnsparger said. 'It meant they had to throw more. Tarkenton is a great passer, a great quarterback, but if you know a quarterback has to throw, it makes it easier to defend against him.' The Dolphins added a Garo Yepremian field goal in the second quarter and took a 17-0 half-time lead. The third quarter brought another killer drive and Csonka's second touchdown, a two-yard run to end an eight-play drive. The 238-pound fullback was named the game's Most Valuable Player. His 145 yards rushing set a new Super Bowl record. A farm boy who had broken the career rushing record at Syracuse University (surpassing Jim Brown, Floyd Little, Ernie Davis and Jim Nance) the 27-year-old Csonka relished the role of running back. 'It's nice,' he said of opposing linemen and linebackers, 'to know that you're punishing these guys as much as they're punishing you. . . . You can hear the noise of the clack of equipment and you can see their eyes peering at you through their facemasks and their hands clawing for you. With good blocking, you know you're getting away from them, and even for a few yards that's exciting.'

Jack Patera, the Viking defensive line coach, admitted he was impressed by the performance of Csonka and his line. 'It's the most well-coordinated offensive team I've ever seen,' Patera told reporters, adding that he had studied and restudied films hop-

Right: *This was another good day for Miami's remarkable Garo Yepremian, who kicked a 28-yard field goal and all of his team's three extra points.*

Far right: *Game stats cannot really convey the importance of Bob Griese's fine tactics to Miami's victory in SB VIII.*

ing to come up with a way to stop the Miami offense from running over them the way it had over other teams. 'But we thought maybe some of those other teams like Cincinnati or Oakland didn't prepare for them properly. We took great pains to prepare for this game, but they went out and did the same thing to us.' Tarkenton was stoic about the outcome. 'You play the game at great risk,' he said. 'We went out and gave it a shot and weren't good enough.... They are an excellent team and played as near to perfect as you can play.'

Monte Clark, coach of the Dolphin offensive line, was ecstatic over the unit's performance. 'We thought it would be tough to get outside their defensive ends because they're so wide-conscious,' he said. 'So we wanted to run inside more, but to do that we had to fool them into thinking we might be going wide, or trapping them so that there'd be a hole.'

One of the more interesting battles in the trenches pitted Miami guard Bob Keuchenberg against his former Notre Dame teammate, Alan Page. 'He was a little annoyed,' Keuchenberg said of Page. 'He was saying a lot of things out there.... Alan made a couple of big plays, too. You can't stop a player like Alan Page on every play.'

As it had been since Super Bowl I, the players on the winning team collected $15,000 each, the losers $7500. It seemed the Dolphins might dominate for years to come, but a glitch developed in the grand scheme of things. Bill Arnsparger, the defensive genius, left to become coach of the New York Giants. 'The Giants are getting a great coach,' Shula said. Even worse, the World Football League held its organizational meeting the day after the Super Bowl, and by March the Toronto Northmen of the new league had signed Csonka, Kiick and Paul Warfield to contracts. Although Csonka and Warfield played with the Dolphins in 1974, the championship atmosphere had been shattered. The WFL completed one season, then gasped and died in the middle of the next, surviving just long enough to dismantle one of pro football's truly great teams.

Super Bowl

IX

Pittsburgh Steelers 16, Minnesota Vikings 6

12 January 1975
Tulane Stadium, New Orleans
Attendance: 80,997

Pittsburgh	0	2	7	7	—	16
Minnesota	0	0	0	6	—	6

Pittsburgh – Safety, White downed Tarkenton in end zone.
Pittsburgh – Harris, 9, run (Gerela kick).
Minnesota – T Brown recovered blocked punt in end zone (kick failed).
Pittsburgh – L Brown, 4, pass from Bradshaw (Gerela kick).

Rushing: *Pittsburgh* – Harris, 34 for 158, 1 TD; Bleier, 17 for 65; Bradshaw, 5 for 33; Swann, 1 for –7. *Minnesota* – Foreman, 12 for 18; Tarkenton, 1 for 0; Osborn, 8 for –1.
Passing: *Pittsburgh* – Bradshaw, 9 of 14 for 97, 1 TD. *Minnesota* – Tarkenton, 11 of 26, for 102, 3 int.
Receiving: *Pittsburgh* – Brown, 3 for 49, 1 TD; Stallworth, 3 for 24; Bleier, 2 for 11; Lewis, 1 for 12. *Minnesota* – Foreman, 5 for 50; Voigt, 2 for 31; Osborn, 2 for 7; Gilliam, 1 for 16; Reed, 1 for –2.
Punting: *Pittsburgh* – Walden, 7 for 34.7 average. *Minnesota* – Eischeid, 6 for 37.2.
Punt Returns: *Pittsburgh* – Swann, 3 for 34; Edwards, 2 for 2. *Minnesota* – McCullum, 3 for 11; N Wright, 1 for 1.
Kickoff Returns: *Pittsburgh* – Harrison, 2 for 17; Pearson, 1 for 15. *Minnesota* – McCullum, 1 for 26; McClanahan, 1 for 22; B Brown, 1 for 2.
Interceptions: *Pittsburgh* – Wagner, 1 for 26; Blount, 1 for 10; Greene, 1 for 10. *Minnesota* – None.

Super Bowl IX. Viking QB Fran Tarkenton prepares to pass as Steeler Ernie Holmes closes in.

Just when football fans had settled in with the notion that the Miami Dolphins would be the dynasty of the 1970s, the Pittsburgh Steelers stepped in and complicated the picture. In retrospect, the two franchises were in a rigorous struggle to see which would emerge. By appearing in three straight Super Bowls, the Dolphins had seemed the early favorite. But the Miami franchise, weakened by a talent drain from the World Football League, stumbled slightly in 1974. And the Steelers, a young team brimming with ability, seized the opportunity and squeezed from it four Super Bowl championships, settling in many minds the question of the decade's dominant team.

In defense of Don Shula and his Dolphins, it should be pointed out that they did not go gentle into their goodnight. Their 1974 AFC playoff collision with John Madden's Oakland Raiders had been billed by a network PR man as 'the real Super Bowl.' Justified, perhaps, although neither team eventually made it. It could be argued that both reached the zenith of competition in their playoff meeting in Oakland-Alameda County Coliseum. It was a marvelous game, with the two teams fighting throughout for the lead as if it were some precious stone. Miami scored, then Oakland, then Miami for a 10-7 edge at half-time. The third quarter resumed at the same pace. Oakland scored to take the lead, then Miami again and again to nose ahead at 19-14. Oakland quickly jumped back at 21-19.

By the two and a half minute mark of the fourth quarter, Bob Griese had returned the Dolphins to the Oakland 23. The Raiders were caught napping with Benny Malone's 23-yard run up the middle – 26-21, Miami. Shula knew the 2:08 left on the clock was too much. Oakland quarterback Ken 'Snake' Stabler confirmed it with two quick passes to Fred Biletnikoff, then two more to Cliff Branch and Frank Pitts. Raider running back Clarence Davis then knifed inside to the Miami eight. Just 35 seconds remained. Snake burned his last timeout, talked things over with Madden and receiver coach Tom Flores, then attempted a flare pass. The receivers were covered, he scrambled, and just as Dolphins defensive end Vern Den Herder pulled him down, Stabler cut loose with a desperate dead duck to Clarence Davis in the end zone. The Raiders dropped the Dolphin dynasty in its tracks, 28-26. It would take Shula nearly a decade to recover.

Immediately the football world was hit with the idea that the Raiders would be the team. Nothing infuriated Pittsburgh coach Chuck Noll more. 'The Raiders think they can't be beat,' he said in the days before the AFC championship game. 'But we're going out there and kick their butt.'

The hurt was still with the Steelers from their 33-14 loss to the Raiders in the 1973 playoffs. Pittsburgh returned to Oakland for the '74 championship and for the first three quarters, Noll's prediction seemed in peril. The Raiders led, 10-3, until Terry Bradshaw and the Steelers zipped off 21 fourth-quarter points to win, 24-13.

Suddenly, the moment Pittsburgh owner Art

Opposite top: *Steeler QB Terry Bradshaw lofts one.*

Opposite below: *Viking Fran Tarkenton downed for a safety.*

Left: *Steeler RB Franco Harris plunges through the line.*

Above: *Steeler defenders help Tarkenton to his feet.*

Rooney waited 39 years for had arrived. The Steelers were going to the NFL championship game. Countless times, he had anguished watching his team mired in losing seasons. The first real inkling of a turnaround hadn't come until 1968, when Pittsburgh hired Noll, then a Baltimore assistant coach, to reverse the team's miserable fortunes. It took a few seasons and some brilliant and lucky draft selections. But it happened. The Steelers would go on to win four Super Bowls between 1974 and 1980, and to say they did it in 'blue-collar' fashion would be more than a bit trite. Yet there's hardly a way around it. In the age of America's great industrial decline, the Steelers became a lingering symbol of potency. They were hard, polished Pittsburgh steel, running roughshod over the competition with a defense led by Mean Joe Greene, Jack Lambert, LC Greenwood, Jack Ham and Mel Blount. The offense had a similar cast with running backs Rocky Bleier and Franco Harris and quarterback Terry Bradshaw. The sassy style was added by receivers Lynn Swann and John Stallworth. They were mere rookies in 1974. But as the other draft picks ahead of them, they would go on to greatness, paying the Pittsburgh management tremendous dividends.

After getting close but being denied by Miami in 1972 and Oakland in 1973, Noll's Steelers found their stride over the 1974 season, although it wasn't easy. The Steelers won all six of their preseason games and Joe Gilliam, one of modern football's early black quarterbacks, clearly beat out Bradshaw for the starting job. But Noll switched quarterbacks in midseason as the Steelers were on their way to a 10-3-1 finish. The knock against Bradshaw was that while he had a great arm, some critics suggested that he wasn't smart enough to direct the team's offense. For the most part, the quarterback endured this criticism in silence.

In the NFC, the Minnesota Vikings fought their way out of the pack for the third time and second consecutive year. Their basic structure was the same, with a strong defense and quarterback Fran Tarkenton running a versatile offense. Using just that, they finished the regular season 10-4, then bumped St Louis and quarterback Jim Hart in the first round of the playoffs, 30-14. The difference was a 16-point third quarter in which both the offense and defense contributed touchdowns. On the day Tarkenton passed for 169 yards and Chuck Foreman rushed for 114.

The Los Angeles Rams, having knocked off wildcard Washington in the playoffs for their first playoff victory since 1952, met Minnesota for the NFC title. As forecast, the match was a defensive battle. The

Rams turned the ball over five times, the Vikings three. But Minnesota sustained two drives for touchdowns to win, 14-10.

NFL officials had hoped the Louisiana Superdome would be finished in time for Super Bowl IX, but construction delays meant the game would be played in Tulane Stadium once again. Regardless, the city of New Orleans was ready with a party.

The pressure, of course, was on the Vikings. For the most part, they seemed confident of their chances. 'This is the third time we've competed in the Super Bowl,' said Beverley Osborn, wife of Minnesota running back Dave Osborn, 'and I just have a gut feeling that we won't walk away losers again. Dave didn't talk much before he left for New Orleans, but I could tell he was confident in himself and his teammates.'

Many prognosticators felt the Pittsburgh power game would present the Vikings with the same kind of problems they had faced against Miami and Csonka in Super Bowl VIII. As things turned out, that's exactly what happened, although it took a while for any discernible pattern to emerge from the play in Super Bowl IX. Early morning rains had made Tulane Stadium's artificial turf a slick, wet car-

Top left: *Pittsburgh WR Lynn Swann, still a rookie in Super Bowl IX, would come into his own the next year.*

Left: *Viking QB Fran Tarkenton hands off to RB Chuck Foreman.*

Above: *Viking RB Dave Osborn carries behind the blocking of guard Ed White.*

pet, and by game time, the wind was whipping with a 20-degree chill factor, a development that further tipped the scale toward defense and a solid ground game. The weather piled on Minnesota's poor luck. The Vikings won the opening coin toss and decided to kick with the wind at their backs. But by kickoff time, the gusts had shifted into their faces and lined up with the Pittsburgh offense.

The only scoring of the first half came at the 7:49 mark of the second quarter when Tarkenton attempted a pitchout deep in his own territory, fumbled and fell on the ball in the end zone. Later the Vikings drove to the Pittsburgh goal, but Minnesota receiver John Gilliam was hit while making a reception and the ball popped out to Steeler defensive back Mel Blount for a touchdown-saving interception.

'I saw John Gilliam coming across out of the corner of my eye,' said Steeler defensive back Glen Edwards, who made the hit to cause the interception. 'I knew I had to give him a blow and hope he would cough the ball up. Five times out of 10 they'll cough it up, and he coughed it up.' The Steelers carried a 2-0 lead from the safety into the locker room at the half.

Things turned even more sour for the Vikings from

there when Bill Brown fumbled the second half kick-off. Four plays later, Franco Harris scored on a nine-yard run to give the Steelers a 9-0 lead. Tired of waiting on the offense to accomplish something, the Minnesota defense finally heated up some momentum early in the fourth quarter. The Vikings' offense had gotten a first down at the Pittsburgh five on a pass interference call, but Foreman fumbled on the next play and the Steelers recovered. Four plays later, when Pittsburgh attempted to punt, the Vikings' Matt Blair blocked it and Terry Brown recovered in the end zone for a Minnesota touchdown. When Viking kicker Fred Cox missed the conversion, the Steelers led, 9-6.

Pittsburgh began a drive from there and headed into Viking territory. The drive seemed to stall when Steeler tight end Larry Brown apparently fumbled at the Viking 28, but the officials ruled the ball was

dead. The call incensed Vikings coach Bud Grant. 'From our vantage point,' Grant said, 'Brown had not reached the ground when the ball came loose. Our bench reacted immediately. There wasn't any question in their mind that it was a fumble, but the officials ruled the ball dead. But that's the way the game went – it was just a succession of errors by all three teams.'

The Steelers went on to finish off the drive and the Vikings with a four-yard touchdown pass from Bradshaw to Brown, providing the final margin, 16-6. The Vikings' disappointment was immediate and obvious. 'It wasn't a very good game,' said Grant, who had become the first coach to lose three Super Bowl games. 'Neither team got here playing this kind of football. There was enough chances for both teams to win a number of times with all the penalties, interceptions and fumbles.'

Tarkenton, however, refused to be glum or make excuses. 'Their defense was simply too good,' he said. 'If Sandy Koufax is pitching, you don't score too many runs. . . . We came to win and we couldn't do it. They were the better football team. They deserved to win. They did it, we didn't.'

The big story of the game was Harris' record 158 yards rushing on 34 carries, enough to earn him the Most Valuable Player award. 'I was surprised I had that many yards,' Harris said afterward, 'but I wasn't thinking about it that much either. I had a head cold, but you can't let a cold stop you. There's no cure for it anyway.'

Noll was just as pleased with his defense, particularly a recently installed alignment that placed tackles Ernie Holmes and Joe Greene in tight over the center. 'It confuses their offensive blocking scheme,' Noll explained. 'I can't think of anything more fitting than for our defense to shut them out.'

Mean Joe Greene was even happier, telling reporters, 'Even in my wildest dreams I didn't think I'd get as big a charge out of winning the Super Bowl as I have. I'm a fan. And every Super Bowl day in the past, I sat there watching it on TV and envying the guys that won. And today I was there. And I was happy for Chuck Noll and the whole team because we've really had the highs and lows this season. And this is what makes it so nice.'

The Steelers' quarterback, who completed 9 of 14 attempts for 96 yards and a touchdown and who rushed for another 33 yards, felt his own sense of accomplishment – and relief. 'I've faced a lot of adversity,' Bradshaw said. 'I withstood the trials and that enabled me, that and my personal faith in God, to do this. I've looked at all sides being a hero and being a jerk. I think I can handle winning the Super Bowl very well.'

The real unsung hero of the day was Pittsburgh equipment manager Tony Parisi, who had acquired 75 pairs of non-skid, rubber-cleated shoes for the game. It was a trick he had learned from the Miami Dolphins' equipment man after Miami defeated Pittsburgh on wet artificial turf several years earlier. 'God knows where he found those shoes, but a lot of us wore them and it was as if they came from heaven,' said Steeler linebacker Andy Russell, the winners' defensive captain.

As time would show, heaven would do a bit more smiling upon the Steelers over the next few years.

Left: *Steeler RB Franco Harris.*

Top Inset: *Steeler Joe Greene pursues Tarkenton.*

Bottom Inset: *Rocky Bleier.*

68
68

Super Bowl X

Pittsburgh Steelers 21, Dallas Cowboys 17

18 January 1976
Orange Bowl, Miami
Attendance: 80,187

Dallas	7	3	0	7	—	17
Pittsburgh	7	0	0	14	—	21

Dallas – D Pearson, 29, pass from Staubach (Fritsch kick).
Pittsburgh – Grossman, 7, pass from Bradshaw (Gerela kick).
Dallas – Field goal, 36, Fritsch.
Pittsburgh – Safety, Harrison blocked Hoopes' punt through end zone.
Pittsburgh – Field goal, 36, Gerela.
Pittsburgh – Field goal, 18, Gerela.
Pittsburgh – Swann, 64, pass from Bradshaw (kick failed).
Dallas – P Howard, 34, pass from Staubach (Fritsch kick).

Rushing: *Dallas* – Newhouse, 16 for 56; Staubach, 5 for 22; Dennison, 5 for 16; Pearson, 5 for 14. *Pittsburgh* – Harris, 27 for 82; Bleier, 15 for 51; Bradshaw, 4 for 16.
Passing: *Dallas* – Staubach, 15 of 24 for 204, 2 TD, 3 int. *Pittsburgh* – Bradshaw, 9 of 19 for 209, 2 TD.
Receiving: *Dallas* – P Pearson, 5 for 53; Young, 3 for 31; D Pearson, 2 for 59, 1 TD; Newhouse, 2 for 12; P Howard, 1 for 34, 1 TD; Fugett, 1 for 9; Dennison, 1 for 6. *Pittsburgh* – Swann, 4 for 161, 1 TD; Stallworth, 2 for 8; Harris, 1 for 26; Grossman, 1 for 7; L Brown, 1 for 7.
Punting: *Dallas* – Hoopes, 7 for 35.0 average. *Pittsburgh* – Walden, 4 for 39.8.
Punt Returns: *Dallas* – Richards, 1 for 5. *Pittsburgh* – D Brown, 3 for 14; Edwards, 2 for 17.
Kickoff Returns: *Dallas* – T Henderson, 48, after lateral; P Pearson, 4 for 48. *Pittsburgh* – Blount, 3 for 64; Collier, 1 for 25.
Interceptions: *Dallas* – None. *Pittsburgh* – Edwards, 1 for 35; Thomas, 1 for 35; Wagner, 1 for 19.

Super Bowl X. This Steeler-Cowboy duel was hailed as the best Super Bowl thus far.

SUPER BOWL X

Right, top and center: *Dallas fans wanted a win like that over Minnesota in the wildcard playoffs. It was not to be.*

Right bottom: *Rookie Dallas LB Thomas Henderson.*

The 1975 season offered the fans an unexpected amalgam of prayer passes, wild-card chances and good old power football. When all was said and done, the Pittsburgh Steelers had set another stone in the foundation of their dynasty.

But probably the season's real thrills came in Dallas, where the Cowboys were expected to have a rebuilding year following the retirement of defensive tackle Bob Lilly, running back Walt Garrison and defensive back Cornell Green. Insult piled on injury when running back Calvin Hill jumped to the World Football League. Somehow Tom Landry and Roger Staubach coaxed the young team to a 10-4 record and a wild-card playoff spot.

Their first-round game at Metropolitan Stadium in Minneapolis would bring the ultimate expression of Minnesota's playoff misfortunes. The '75 Vikings were their usual veteran, balanced selves. Having compiled a 12-2 regular season record, they were eager to return to the Super Bowl for a third straight year and secure the trophy. A cynic would have said that the up-and-down Cowboys didn't have a prayer. The day, of course, would prove differently. The Cowboys, in fact, had several prayers. Their late-game miracle would provide the NFL with a Ave Maria for posterity.

The Vikings recovered a fumbled punt in the second quarter and used the field position to take a 7-0 halftime lead. Dallas evened things up with a third-quarter drive, then took the lead on a Toni Fritsch field goal just minutes into the fourth quarter.

Facing the challenge of the season, Fran Tarkenton pulled the Vikings together for a 70-yard drive in 11 plays. Brent McClanahan powered in from the one to make the game 14-10, Minnesota. Faced with a similar challenge, the Cowboy offense fizzled and punted with about three minutes left. The answer would lie with the defense, which had been bolstered with a crop of rookies – Randy White, Herb Scott, Bob Breunig, Thomas Henderson. The telling moment came as Minnesota faced a third and two at the Cowboy 47. Tarkenton eschewed the dive for a rollout.

Dallas safety Charlie Waters blitzed and dropped him for a three-yard loss. Reluctantly, the Vikings punted.

The Dallas offense again fizzled. The last hope hinged on a fourth and 16 situation at their own 25. Roger Staubach and receiver Drew Pearson decided to fake a post pattern and angle for the sideline. The momentum of the pass probably would have carried Pearson out of bounds for an incompletion. But he was bumped by cornerback Nate Wright, and the official ruled Pearson had been forced out of bounds. With 37 seconds left, Dallas had a first down at the 50. When the next pass fell incomplete, Pearson said it was time to work on Wright long again. The pass was short, bringing Pearson back from the end zone to catch it. As he moved to the ball, Wright fell, or as the Vikings claimed, he was knocked down by offensive interference. Pearson caught the ball at the five, clutched it to his waist, then felt it slipping away as he fell into the end zone. With the ball pinned awkwardly at his hip, Pearson glanced around for penalty flags. There was none, only the dead silence of Metropolitan Stadium. The play became enshrined as 'Hail Mary,' and has become over the years one of the game's hallowed moments.

For the Cowboys, the next step came the following week against the favored Los Angeles Rams. Dallas, however, wasted little time in running over the Rams, 37-7. For the first time in the game's 10-year history, a wild-card team had reached the Super Bowl.

Top: *Both of Dallas' TDs were made on passes from QB Roger Staubach (12).*

Above: *Staubach hands off to Preston Pearson as Steeler DE Dwight White closes in.*

For Pittsburgh, the 1975 season is remembered for the emergence of second-year receiver Lynn Swann, a wisp of gentility amid the Pittsburgh Steelers' brutality. Or at least that was his image, an image, of course, that began with his name. The sportswriters immediately reached for descriptions of grace and splendor. Swann surely was all of those things. He could run, he could leap, he could catch, all with a style to match his name.

Swann and fellow receiver John Stallworth were mere rookies when the Steelers had used their defensive viciousness to subdue the Minnesota Vikings, 16-6, in Super Bowl IX. By the next season, Swann had matured into one of the game's truly gifted pass catchers. Teamed with Stallworth, he opened up the Steeler offense and helped lead the team to a consecutive Super Bowl appearance. Over the course of the regular season, Swann caught 49 passes for 781 yards and 11 touchdowns. Quarterback Terry Bradshaw threw for 2055 yards and 18 touchdowns as the Steelers posted a 12-2 record.

In the first round of the playoffs, Pittsburgh easily dismissed the Baltimore Colts, 28-10. But the AFC title game against the Oakland Raiders was a slugfest. The Steelers won, 16-10, but in the third period Swann collapsed after being nailed by Raider safety George Atkinson. Doctors diagnosed a concussion and kept Swann for observation. Immediately, questions were raised about Swann's ability to play against the Dallas Cowboys in the Super Bowl two weeks away. Yet within a week, Swann had returned to a limited participation in practice. As it became more apparent he would play in the Super Bowl, the Cowboys began speculating on his effectiveness. Would the head injury make him gun shy? Swann

admitted some doubt. 'I thought about it,' he told reporters before the game. 'But finally I said the heck with it. I'm going out there and playing 100 percent.'

His health was just one of several central themes batted around by the media in the days before the game at Miami's Orange Bowl. A record 1735 media people requested credentials for the game, leading the *New York Times* to comment: 'To escape mention of the Super Bowl in the next eight days one must almost resign from the human race. . . . Less enthusiastic sociologists have described the Super Bowl as America's number one symbol of excess.'

The NFL was pleased with the growth to say the least. Its television and radio rights fees had grown to $3.8 million, which seemed to be an astronomical figure at the time.

For the first time, the press centered its attention on Pittsburgh's excellent linebacking corps – Jack Ham, Jack Lambert and Andy Russell. 'I like the front four,' coach Paul Wiggin of Kansas City commented when asked for his analysis, 'and I like the secondary. But when it comes right down to it, I love those linebackers. They're sensational!'

Green Bay coach Bart Starr was queried as to what strategic changes the two teams might make. 'You get there,' Starr replied, 'by being sound and running very successful programs. In a game like that, you go with what got you there. You might make a slight change to take advantage of an individual's idiosyncrasies, but that's all.' Held on 18 January 1976, the Super Bowl was one of the first major events to kick off America's Bicentennial celebration. Accordingly, the coin toss to start the game made use of a three-inch-thick Bicentennial medal, weighing nearly a pound and costing about $4000.

Opposite top: *Steeler Franco Harris again led in rushing, but his 82 yards paled beside his 158 of the year before.*

Opposite below: *Staubach hands off to Robert Newhouse. In the game Staubach passed for 204 and rushed for 22.*

Above: *Dallas' Mitch Hoopes had an end-zone punt blocked for a safety. (Beyond Hoopes in this shot: Jack Lambert.)*

Left: *Steeler RB Rocky Bleier.*

The Cowboys used Staubach and their shotgun offense to blast to a 7-0 lead. Then Swann stoked the Steelers' first scoring drive with a leaping, acrobatic catch of a Bradshaw pass at the Dallas 16. Somehow, he had retrieved the ball in midair from sailing incomplete out of bounds, then he twisted to land inbounds. Good for 32 yards, the play set up a scoring pass to tight end Randy Grossman moments later. Dallas added a 36-yard field goal in the second quarter. The teams traded possessions thereafter, leaving the Cowboys clinging to a 10-7 lead until three minutes into the fourth quarter when Pittsburgh's Reggie Harrison blocked Mitch Hoopes' punt out of the end zone for a safety. With that, the Steelers pulled to 10-9.

'I had my hands up like this on his second step,' Harrison said afterward. 'He wasn't gonna kick that ball. I don't know where the ball hit me. I thought I blocked it with my arms but my tongue is split down the middle and I think it hit me in the mouth. It didn't hurt much. I was yellin' and screamin' so when I went to the bench, I didn't realize we got any points.'

'I didn't see him until I was kicking the ball,' said Hoopes, the rookie punter, who had only one of 68 punts blocked during the regular season. 'No, I wasn't slow on it. What can you say? There's nothing you can do. It makes me sick.'

Forced to kick after the safety, the Cowboys watched the Steelers' Mike Collier return the kick 25 yards, setting up a Roy Gerela field goal for a 12-10 Steeler lead. The scene worsened moments later when Mike Wagner intercepted Staubach's pass to set up yet another Gerela field goal and a 15-10 Pittsburgh lead.

Minutes later from their own 36, Bradshaw and Swann opted for the bomb. Swann set sail, and Bradshaw lofted a fat one for him to run under. The result was another elegant passage in Swann's highlight poem: a 64-yard gamebuster for a 21-10 lead. The point after failed. On the down side, Bradshaw was knocked silly by the Dallas rush on the play and lost for the rest of the game.

Staubach brought the Cowboys right back with a quick touchdown pass, then got the ball back again trailing 21-17. But the Steel Curtain defense closed out the Dallas performance by intercepting Staubach's final Hail Mary attempt.

The MVP trophy belonged to Swann, who had caught four passes for 161 yards. 'Until yesterday,' Swann said, 'I felt stiff. I couldn't get loose. I had no concentration.'

'That's right,' Bradshaw commented. 'He couldn't catch a cold.'

'I couldn't have played a week ago,' Swann continued, 'But once I felt all right yesterday, I thought I'd be all right for the game. When a ball player is

Left: *Steeler Roy Gerala (10) kicks his second field goal.*

Right: *Steeler WR Lynn Swann caught for 161 and one TD.*

Left: *Bradshaw hands off to Bleier. Visible on the Steeler line are guard Jim Clack (50) and tackle Jon Kolb (55).*

Bottom: *Coach Tom Landry and the Cowboys.*

hurt, it's like falling off a horse. You question yourself until you play again. I wanted to have a good game for myself.'

Asked for his comments, Tom Landry, the Dallas coach, said, 'The blocked punt changed the momentum. It cost us five points and that was the difference. That Lynn Swann was really something. He made two big catches when he was covered.'

The day had been rough for Staubach. The Steelers had sacked him a Super Bowl record seven times and intercepted three of his passes. 'Pittsburgh is the best,' he said.

With the win, Pittsburg coach Chuck Noll joined the coaching elite of the NFL – Vince Lombardi and Don Shula – who had two Super Bowl wins each. And for Noll the best was yet to come.

20
23
N. WRIGHT
43
25

Super Bowl XI

Oakland Raiders 32, Minnesota Vikings 14

9 January 1977
Rose Bowl, Pasadena, Calif.
Attendance: 100,421

Oakland	0	16	3	13	—	32
Minnesota	0	0	7	7	—	14

Oakland – Field goal, 24, Mann.
Oakland – Casper, 1, pass from Stabler (Mann kick).
Oakland – Banaszak, 1, run (kick failed).
Oakland – Field goal, 40, Mann.
Minnesota – S White, 8, pass from Tarkenton (Cox kick).
Oakland – Banaszak, 2, run (Mann kick).
Oakland – Brown, 75, interception return (kick failed).
Minnesota – Voigt, 13, pass from Lee (Cox kick).

Rushing: *Oakland* – Davis, 16 for 137; van Eeghen, 18 for 73; Garrett, 4 for 19; Banaszak, 10 for 19, 2 TD; Ginn, 2 for 9; Rae, 2 for 9. *Minnesota* – Foreman, 17 for 44; Johnson, 2 for 9; S White, 1 for 7; Lee, 1 for 4; Miller, 2 for 4; McClanahan, 3 for 3.
Passing: *Oakland* – Stabler, 12 of 19 for 180, 1 TD. *Minnesota* – Tarkenton, 17 of 35 for 205, 2 TD, 1 int; Lee, 7 of 9 for 81, 1 TD.
Receiving: *Oakland* – Biletnikoff, 4 for 79; Casper, 4 for 70, 1 TD; Branch, 3 for 20; Garrett, 1 for 11. *Minnesota* – S White, 5 for 77, 1 TD; Foreman, 5 for 62; Voigt, 4 for 49, 1 TD; Miller, 4 for 19; Rashad, 3 for 53; Johnson, 3 for 26.
Punting: *Oakland* – Guy, 4 for 40.5 average. *Minnesota* – Clabo, 7 for 37.9.
Punt Returns: *Oakland* – Colzie, 4 for 43. *Minnesota* – Willis, 3 for 14.
Kickoff Returns: *Oakland* – Garrett, 2 for 47; Siani, 1 for 0. *Minnesota* – Willis, 3 for 57; S White, 4 for 79.
Interceptions: *Oakland* – Brown, 1 for 75, 1 TD; Hall, 1 for 16. *Minnesota* – None.

Super Bowl XI. Raider WR Fred Biletnikoff tries to run a Ken Stabler pass away from a trio of Viking defenders.

Far left: *Raider safety George Atkinson typified Oakland's 'fire-in-the-belly' spirit.*

Left top: *Oakland coach John Madden.*

Left below: *Viking coach Bud Grant.*

Right above and below: *Two views of Viking Chuck Foreman being downed by defensive end Otis Sistrunk. Rushing and receiving, RB Foreman gained 106 yards on the day.*

Pro football found its stride in the second half of the 1970s. Game attendance had been weakening since 1973, but the league opened two new franchises in 1976 – Seattle and Tampa Bay. With that, a gate draw that had been hovering around 11 million fans per year zoomed off toward 13 million.

The television ratings continued their upward trend as well, lifting with them the league's contracts with the three major networks. The Super Bowl moved from averaging just over 80 million viewers to more than 100 million by the 1980s. A Harris Sports Survey in the mid-seventies reported that 70 percent of the nation's sports fans said they liked pro football, while only 54 percent showed an appreciation for baseball, long billed as the 'national pastime.'

The league signed what was described as the largest television contract in history in 1977. That same year, the league owners signed a five-year collective bargaining agreement with the players' union that put $55 million into their retirement fund.

On the field in 1976, the Oakland Raiders blasted to a 13-1 regular season record behind Ken 'Snake' Stabler's 2737 yards passing and Mark van Eeghen's 1012 yards rushing. The divisional title was their fifth straight and sixth in seven years under coach John Madden. At 40, the 6-foot-4, 250-pound coach had come into his own, having shown that with his football passion and knowledge he had a real ability to manage the sizeable egos around him, from owner Al Davis to his collection of players. Madden had been an assistant coach with the Raiders in the 1960s during their first Super Bowl appearance. When head coach John Rauch retired, Madden was the logical choice to run the team.

'I felt football was going in a different direction,' Davis said of his reason for promoting Madden. 'You could not dominate players like I would like to do. And he knew both offensive and defensive football. He also had a feel for the passing game that we like to use a lot. And he was there, he was on the staff as an assistant coach. I also liked the idea that he was younger than me.'

The string of divisional championships seemed to confirm the wisdom of his choice. Still, the Raiders had always fallen short of making the big game. The 1976 season brought a different feeling, however, as if it would be the year. The only question had been a lopsided loss to the New England Patriots during the regular season. That question arose immediately again in the playoffs, as the Patriots were the first-round opponent. The dark moment came in that first playoff game as New England led, 21-10, heading into the fourth quarter. But the Raiders reached down and came up with two fourth-quarter touchdowns to win, 24-21. On the day, Stabler completed 19 of 32 attempts for 233 yards and a touchdown with no interceptions. The opponents in the AFC title game were the defending world champion Pittsburgh Steelers, who had gotten off to a terrible start, losing four of their first five games, then came on to win nine straight. They had reached the championship game by blitzing Baltimore, 40-14, in the playoffs, but both Franco Harris and Rocky Bleier were injured in that game and were unable to play against the Raiders.

Oakland's 3-4 defense held the denuded Pittsburgh ground game in check, as the Raiders won easily, 24-7. Madden was taking Davis and company to the Super Bowl in Pasedena, California.

In the NFC, the Minnesota Vikings again broke out of the pack, despite the sore knees of aging quarterback Fran Tarkenton. They had run up an 11-2-1 record in winning their division, as Chuck Foreman slashed to 1155 yards on the ground and Tarkenton turned in a stellar passing year (255 of 412 completed for 2961 yards and 17 touchdowns against 8 interceptions). Adding to that offensive potency were receivers Ahmad Rashad and Sammy White, who between them snared 1577 yards in passes. They powered past Washington, 35-20, in the first round of the playoffs as Foreman and Brent McClanahan each rushed for more than 100 yards. In the NFC title game, they dispatched the Los Angeles Rams, 24-13, as Foreman had 118 yards rushing and 81 receiving.

Bud Grant had enjoyed a marvelously successful career as an athlete and coach. He had been a three-sport star at the University of Minnesota, then had gone on to play both pro basketball and football. With the 1976 season, he was 49 and in his tenth year as head coach of the Vikings. In that time, he had taken the expansion team to magnificent heights. With the win over the Rams, he was taking them to their fourth Super Bowl, having lost the previous three. He had a knack for hiding his loose, easy-going personality behind a stone-faced tact. When asked about the prospects for this fourth Super Bowl appearance, he said simply, 'It should be a great game. It will be played on grass, and both these teams prefer grass. It should be a good field, and we should have good weather. We know we've got good teams.'

Despite Grant's humble approach, the other team offered just the opposite image, and no one typified that Raider ruthlessness better than defensive back

12

Left: *Raider QB Ken 'Snake' Stabler led the NFL in passing in 1976. If he only passed for 180 in SB XI it was because the whole Raider offense so totally dominated Minnesota.*

Right: *Raider Fred Biletnikoff was the game's MVP. He entered the Hall of Fame in 1987.*

Right below: *Clarence Davis, Oakland RB, was the leading rusher of the day at 137. The fact that this was more than three times the yardage gained by the Vikings' rush leader may tell us something.*

George Atkinson. 'Maybe this time,' Atkinson said when asked about the Super Bowl. 'I want to cop the Super Bowl. Oh how I want that! It's been such a long time. Would you believe I've been in eight championship playoffs?'

In the opening game of the season, the Raiders had beaten the Steelers, 31-28, and Pittsburgh receiver Lynn Swann, who was covered by Atkinson, had sustained a concussion, leading Steeler coach Chuck Noll to complain about the 'criminal element' in the league. The league fined Atkinson $1500 for his actions on the field and Noll $1000 for his talk afterwards. Atkinson filed a $1 million slander suit against Noll and against an Oakland newspaper columnist. 'I'm not out to hurt anybody,' Atkinson told reporters before the Super Bowl. 'I don't play angry. I play a controlled game. I'm an intense player. Intimidation is important. If I can break the other man's concentration, I've got an edge on him. Remember, they're mostly bigger than me. I'm six feet, 185, and there are many forms of intimidation. Howard Cosell practices intimidation. I'm going to hit the other man and he's going to hit me and we both know it. That's the game. If somebody gets injured, that's an accident. I tackle high, that's my style. That stuff about a murder rap . . . Well, if the hit I gave Swann would kill, I'd have three for four dead every day, receivers and linemen, too.'

That intimidation factor and the size advantage the Raiders enjoyed on their offensive line, led by the great 6-foot-5, 280-pound Art Shell at tackle, made the Raiders a six-point favorite. The oddsmakers figured Oakland would run over Shell right at Minnesota's 39-year-old defensive end, Jim Marshall, the smallest in the league at only 217 pounds.

Held at the Rose Bowl, the crowd was the largest in the 11-year history of the Super Bowl. All 103,424 seats were sold out. Figured to be a close game, Super Bowl XI proved to be a mere formality. Oakland devastated Minnesota and in the process set a bevy of Super Bowl records. The game was even more lopsided than the final score, 32-14.

Although the first quarter went scoreless, the Raiders rang up some big numbers, 266 yards rushing and 180 passing. At the half, Oakland led, 16-0, at the third quarter, 19-7. Then the Raiders opened the fourth quarter with two straight touchdowns to blow the doors off the game.

When the game was over, Clarence Davis had rushed for 137 yards, and Fred Biletnikoff had won the MVP Award with four catches for 79 yards, but the win, more than any other Super Bowl, had been a team victory. 'They can't say any more that we don't win the big one,' Madden told his players.

'Now that we're here,' said Biletnikoff, 'we've got the pride. No one is going to knock us off. Next year a lot of people are going to be coming at us. But we had 43 guys fighting harder this year to prove that we had the best team in football and next year we intend to do it again.'

'But I didn't get to vote,' joked Clarence Davis, who had turned in an all-time high with his rushing performance. 'I wasn't surprised we were looking to run. Our offensive linemen don't get too much credit. It shows how good they really are. My yardage came from their blocking.'

Stabler had completed a red-hot playoff string, completing 12 of 19 attempts for 180 yards and a touchdown. 'Stabler,' said Al Davis, 'is like Sandy Koufax: anytime he goes out there he can pitch a no-hitter.'

'Snake called a super game,' said Art Shell. 'He was like a computer. He mixed our passes with the run so well the Vikings couldn't handle us. Now we don't have to spend this off-season with the feeling that we can't win the big one.'

The postgame was a grand time for Davis. He had come to the lowly Raiders in 1963 after a stint as an assistant coach with the San Diego Chargers. In one year, he turned miserable losers into a second place finisher, earning AFL Coach of the Year honors for himself. Through the succession of coaches who followed him – John Rauch, then Madden – Davis had exerted his considerable will in molding a fiercely competitive club. 'When you're writing about me,' he once reportedly told a Raider public relations man, 'use the word "genius".'

Though he had battled the NFL as commissioner of the AFL, and would later fight the league and win the right to move his team to Los Angeles, Davis enjoyed a moment of peace with NFL Commissioner Pete Rozelle following the Super Bowl win. 'Your victory was one of the most impressive in Super Bowl history,' Rozelle told Davis.

'They were magnificent,' Davis said of his team. 'They really were super, magnificent. From an organization standpoint.' Asked if the victory was the payoff for his years of labor, Davis replied, 'I thought it paid off before. I've been having fun a long time. Maybe it's better we didn't win it all before this. You

Below: *Thanks to Oakland LB Phil Villapiano, this pass by Fran Tarkenton will never get aloft. Though he passed for 205, Tarkenton completed only 17 of 35 attempts.*

Left: *Clarence Davis is dumped by Viking LB Jeff Siemon (50).*

Above: *The formidable Oakland backfield in action: QB Ken Stabler (12), RB Pete Banaszak (40), and RB Carl Garrett (31).*

worry about reaching the pinnacle of life too early.'

Atkinson viewed the victory as vindication. 'We went at 'em,' he said. 'If the ball wasn't flying, it was (Tarkenton's) helmet. I was just telling them they're going to get stuck all day. I told them to tell Fran to run a few plays in my area. If you can get the ups on a fella, you get it. That's important.'

The Vikings, meanwhile, had become all too well schooled in making losing, postgame comments. 'We just played them on the wrong day,' Grant said. 'Next time we'll play them on Wednesday. We made one big play (a blocked punt), then we didn't make another for a long time. You have to have them in games like this. Once they got ahead of us they were able to run the ball, which is what everyone tries to do.' The reporters asked Grant if the Raiders were the best team he'd seen all year. 'I'd be crazy if I said no,' he replied. 'They are a great team and they played a great game today and they beat us.'

Jeff Siemon, the Minnesota linebacker who was credited with 15 tackles, didn't mask his feelings. 'They totally dominated us. We have no excuses,' he said. 'I'm disappointed because we may never be in another Super Bowl. Our defense was dog-tired because we were on the field so much. There's no question that exhaustion caught up with all of us.'

The Raiders had held Minnesota to just 77 yards rushing. Forced to pass more, Tarkenton threw for 205 yards, but the figures included two interceptions. He also fumbled at the Oakland two-yard line. 'They dominated us,' said Tarkenton. 'We had perfectly good emotion coming in, but once the game starts you have to have big plays to keep the emotion going and we didn't. The Raiders played extremely well and we played badly.'

Reporters asked if he planned to retire. 'Right now, I can't imagine getting up tomorrow morning,' he said, 'or playing next year. It's the wrong time to ask me. We all retire in January, and feel good again in July.'

60
60
MORTON
7

Super Bowl XII

Dallas Cowboys 27, Denver Broncos 10

15 January 1978
Louisiana Superdome, New Orleans
Attendance: 75,583

Dallas	10	3	7	7	—	27
Denver	0	0	10	0	—	10

Dallas – Dorsett, 3, run (Herrera kick).
Dallas – Field goal, 35, Herrera.
Dallas – Field goal, 43, Herrera.
Denver – Field goal, 47, Turner.
Dallas – Johnson, 45, pass from Staubach (Herrera kick).
Denver – Lytle, 1, run (Turner kick).
Dallas – Richards, 29, pass from Newhouse (Herrera kick).

Rushing: *Dallas* – Dorsett, 15 for 66, 1 TD; Newhouse, 14 for 55; White, 1 for 13; P Pearson, 3 for 11; Staubach, 3 for 6; Laidlaw, 1 for 1; Johnson, 1 for –9. *Denver* – Lytle, 10 for 35, 1 TD; Armstrong, 7 for 27; Weese, 3 for 26; Jensen, 1 for 16; Keyworth, 5 for 9; Perrin, 3 for 8.
Passing: *Dallas* – Staubach, 17 of 25 for 183, 1 TD; Newhouse, 1 of 1 for 29, 1 TD; White, 1 of 2 for 5. *Denver* – Morton, 4 of 15 for 39, 4 int; Weese, 4 of 10 for 22.
Receiving: *Dallas* – P Pearson, 5 for 37; DuPree, 4 for 66; Newhouse, 3 for –1; Johnson, 2 for 53, 1 TD; Richards, 2 for 38, 1 TD; Dorsett, 2 for 11; D Pearson, 1 for 13. *Denver* – Dolbin, 2 for 24; Odoms, 2 for 9; Moses, 1 for 21; Upchurch, 1 for 9; Jensen, 1 for 5; Perrin, 1 for –7.
Punting: *Dallas* – White, 5 for 41.6 average, *Denver* – Dilts, 4 for 38.2.
Punt Returns: *Dallas* – Hill, 1 for 1. *Denver* – Upchurch, 3 for 22; Schultz, 1 for 0.
Kickoff Returns: *Dallas* – Johnson, 2 for 29; Brinson, 1 for 22. *Denver* – Upchurch, 3 for 94; Schultz, 2 for 62, Jensen, 1 for 17.
Interceptions: *Dallas* – Washington, 1 for 27; Kyle, 1 for 19; Barnes, 1 for 0; Hughes, 1 for 0. *Denver* – None.

Super Bowl XII. Bronco QB Craig Morton gets set to pass. Blocking are guard Paul Howard (60), and tackle Claudie Minor.

Above: *Cowgirls watch Bronco DE Barney Chavous come out.*

Left: *A fan from outer space.*

The Oakland Raiders had high hopes that they would continue to spread their championship magic over the league in 1977. Added to that hope was their confidence in quarterback Ken 'Snake' Stabler's comeback voodoo, a special potion he had thrown in the faces of opponent's prevent defenses.

He offered the football world another classic example of his spellbinding ability with the Raiders' first-round playoff game against Bert Jones and the Baltimore Colts on Christmas Eve 1977. The regulation was a shootout with Stabler and Jones whipping their offenses up and down the field as the lead changed hands umpteen times. With 14 fourth-quarter points, the Colts took a 31-28 lead with just under two minutes left in the game, but Stabler drove the Raiders to a tying field goal in the closing seconds. The scoring whirlwind died in the first overtime, then the Stabler routine resumed in the sixth period. Efficiently the Raiders moved downfield, where tight end Dave Casper went to the corner of the end zone and pulled in the 10-yard game winner from Stabler, 37-31.

The Raiders' hopes of another special season died the next week in the AFC title game against the upsurging Denver Broncos, led by the veteran Craig Morton. Denver ran out to a 20-3 lead, but Stabler finally found the Raiders' pulse in the fourth quarter with two touchdown passes. A little more time, and they might have won it. Instead, Denver held on for a 20-17 win and a trip to Super Bowl XII.

Denver coach Red Miller had knocked around the league 17 years as an assistant coach before getting his first chance at the top job with the Broncos in 1977. He employed Morton to run his conservative offense, and let the Denver defense do the rest. Fortunately, it was a capable defense with Lyle Alzado, Rubin Carter, Randy Gradishar, Tom Jackson, Louie Wright and Bill Thompson.

Using a mix of luck and moxie, the Broncos had hustled off to a 12-1 start before losing the final regular-season game, 14-6, to the Dallas Cowboys. In the first round of the playoffs, the defense picked off three Terry Bradshaw passes, and the offense made no major mistakes, as Miller's bunch eliminated Pittsburgh, 34-21. That and the victory the next week over Oakland had made believers of the skeptics.

'Our players are in good frame of mind,' Miller said in a press conference before the Super Bowl. 'They're loose. They want to play well. . . . On paper and stats-wise, Dallas is better than we are but we had that happen lots of times this year and just outplayed 'em. If we can win the individual matchups, we've got a helluva chance. I think our X's and O's will be all right but I want the mental part to be right for every individual. Too many coaches have too much ego, think too much of their own importance. I feel it's the players who are important and I'm here only to help 'em pull together.'

Above: *Denver defenders Rubin Carter (68), Randy Gradishar (53) and Tom Jackson (57).*

Left: *LB Tom Jackson* vs *Dallas RB Tony Dorsett.*

Racked by dissension the previous year when John Ralston had been their coach, the Broncos had responded to Miller's laid-back approach by earning the first championship appearance in the team's 17-year history. In Denver, where Broncomania was raging, it became the season of the 'Orange Crush' defense. Seldom in the history of pro sports has a community responded to a team the way Denver did for the Broncos.

A central figure in the success was the 35-year-old Morton, who despite nagging hip injuries through much of the late season, had given the team just the taste of experienced offense it needed. During the regular season, he completed 131 of 254 passes for 1929 yards and 14 touchdowns against eight interceptions. In the playoffs, he had thrown four more touchdown passes and only one interception. The storybook season added a mean twist to its plot when

Morton's old team, the Dallas Cowboys, emerged as the Broncos' Super Bowl opponent. In the NFC, the Cowboys had added to the Minnesota Vikings' playoff woes by beating them, 23-6, in the title game. With Roger Staubach, the Dallas passing game was as impressive as ever over the 1977 season as Landry's team finished 12-2. But the Cowboys had a new edge in their backfield with rookie back Tony Dorsett, their number one draft choice out of the University of Pittsburgh. Landry brought him along slowly, but once given the chance to play, Dorsett had contributed immediately, gaining 1007 yards his first season.

The Dallas sports media questioned Dorsett's fat contract. 'I don't care if he gets $2 million as long as he helps us get to the Super Bowl this season,' Roger Staubach said. 'But if we don't get there, he's got to give $1 million of it back.' Reaching the Super Bowl his first season only confirmed Dorsett's value to the franchise. 'Playing with the best and against the best,' he said, 'It brings out the best in you. I think it was a good season for myself, but I think it will take me two or three years to know all that I should about the game.'

Asked about Landry's decision to play Preston Pearson ahead of him in the early games, Dorsett replied, 'I was disappointed, yes, being the type of athlete I am. But I think the coach brought me along in fine fashion. And the type of person Preston is made it easier for me to accept.'

'My timing was not the best,' Landry said of his midseason shift to Dorsett, 'but I felt it had to be done then to have Tony ready for the playoffs.'

Without question, the Broncos saw Dorsett as a major factor. 'I don't think they'll run him outside as much as they'll try to pop him through holes,' said Tom Jackson, the Broncos' linebacker. 'But we can't let him get us in a foot race. He's too fast for that.

Far left: *Dallas' Tony Dorsett made the game's first score, a three-yard first-quarter TD.*

Above: *Dallas' Roger Staubach passed for almost five times as much yardage as his Denver counterpart, Craig Morton.*

Left: *The Cowgirls cheer the departing Staubach at halftime.*

Left: *Teammates congratulate Dallas WR Butch Johnson after his 45-yard TD run on a pass from Staubach.*

Right: *Dallas reserve QB Danny White downed by LB Bob Swenson.*

When we played them four weeks ago, it took me a quarter to adjust to his speed. He can come to a full stop, then be at full speed in one step.'

The Super Bowl hype was built around the two old Dallas quarterbacking foes, Morton and Staubach, coming face to face. The real difference, however, turned on Dallas' formidable 'flex defense,' featuring Ed 'Too Tall' Jones, Harvey Martin, Jethro Pugh, Randy White, Hollywood Henderson, D D Lewis, Bob Breunig, Charlie Waters and Cliff Harris.

Played in the Louisiana Superdome, the game was the first Super Bowl held inside, a development that made NFL Commissioner Pete Rozelle a bit nostalgic. 'I'm going to miss the balloons,' he said of the pre-game color when the event was played under the open sky. 'I love seeing the balloons go up in the sky.' Instead, the pre-game show featured a group of girls from a Texas junior college, a session with jazz clarinetist Pete Fountain and the antics of two dogs that could catch Frisbees.

It didn't matter, at least not for the Broncos. Everything Morton had accomplished over the season was reversed in the first half. The Cowboys quickly lowered the roof on Denver. Under heavy pressure, Morton was sacked several times and threw four first-half interceptions, as Dallas took a 13-0 lead. To that they added big scoring plays in the third and fourth quarters, ending things up at 27-10. The Cowboys had their second world title. Staubach had completed 17 of 25 passing attempts for 183 yards and a touchdown. Running back Robert Newhouse had thrown an option pass 29 yards for another score.

But the tenor of the victory had been sung by the Doomsday defense, particularly the pass rush. Accordingly, tackle Randy White and defensive end Harvey Martin were selected co-MVPs, the only time in the history of the Super Bowl that the award has been shared. 'We had a great pass rush,' Landry said. 'The defense was super. They gave us so many opportunities in the first half that we could have put the game away then.'

But the Dallas offense had stalled and seemed tentative, coming up with only 13 points despite Denver's seven first-half turnovers. 'I was concerned,' Landry said. 'But when you're playing a great defensive team, you're not going to do the things you can do against another team. We were so high at first that we couldn't do anything; we were making mistakes and everything. But then we settled down.'

'That's happened to us numerous times this year,' Randy White said of the stalled offense. 'We've had our backs to the wall, but we've always responded and done our job defensively. That's what we did today – we don't depend on anyone to do our job for us. We just go out and do it ourselves.'

The Cowboys' locker room was a bit rowdy over their second title. 'World champions,' shouted linebacker Thomas 'Hollywood' Henderson. 'World champions!'

'Well, it's just a fantastic feeling,' Staubach exclaimed.

Morton had been named NFL Comeback Player of the Year, but it was obvious the title was little consolation after the loss. 'Well, they took away about everything we had,' Morton said. 'I probably did a lot of things I shouldn't have, but their defense was all over me. But we had a great year, and you get this far and you want to come back next year.' Then he paused. 'I'm just upset with myself that I didn't play better in the big one.'

To the champions went the spoils, best of all which was the champion's perspective. 'Beating Denver wasn't easy,' Randy White said. 'A lot of big plays went our way. Everyone tries to make the Super Bowl bigger than it is, but you don't play any differently. It still comes down to who blocks and tackles the best.'

Super Bowl XIII

Pittsburgh Steelers 35, Dallas Cowboys 31

21 January 1979
Orange Bowl, Miami
Attendance: 79,484

Pittsburgh	7	14	0	14	—	35
Dallas	7	7	3	14	—	31

Pittsburgh – Stallworth, 28, pass from Bradshaw (Gerela kick).
Dallas – Hill, 39, pass from Staubach (Septien kick).
Dallas – Hegman, 37, fumble recovery return (Septien kick).
Pittsburgh – Stallworth, 75, pass from Bradshaw (Gerela kick).
Pittsburgh – Bleier, 7, pass from Bradshaw (Gerela kick).
Dallas – Field goal, 27, Septien.
Pittsburgh – Harris, 22, run (Gerela kick).
Pittsburgh – Swann, 18, pass from Bradshaw (Gerela kick).
Dallas – DuPree, 7, pass from Staubach (Septien kick).
Dallas – Johnson, 4, pass from Staubach (Septien kick).

Rushing: *Pittsburgh* – Harris, 20 for 68, 1 TD; Bleier, 2 for 3; Bradshaw, 2 for –5. *Dallas* – Dorsett, 16 for 96; Staubach, 4 for 37; Laidlaw, 3 for 12; P Pearson, 1 for 6; Newhouse, 8 for 3.
Passing: *Pittsburgh* – Bradshaw, 17 of 30 for 318, 4 TD, 1 int. *Dallas* – Staubach, 17 of 30 for 228, 3 TD, 1 int.
Receiving: *Pittsburgh* – Swann, 7 for 124, 1 TD; Stallworth, 3 for 115, 2 TD; Grossman, 3 for 29; Bell, 2 for 21; Harris, 1 for 22; Bleier, 1 for 7, 1 TD. *Dallas* – Dorsett, 5 for 44; D Pearson, 4 for 73; Hill, 2 for 49, 1 TD; Johnson, 2 for 30, 1 TD; DuPree, 2 for 17, 1 TD; P Pearson, 2 for 15.
Punting: *Pittsburgh* – Colquitt, 3 for 43.0 average. *Dallas* – D White, 5 for 39.6.
Punt Returns: *Pittsburgh* – Bell, 4 for 27. *Dallas* – Johnson, 2 for 33.
Kickoff Returns: *Pittsburgh* – L Anderson, 3 for 45. *Dallas* – Johnson, 3 for 63; Brinson, 2 for 41; R White, 1 for 0.
Interceptions: *Pittsburgh* – Blount, 1 for 13. *Dallas* – Lewis, 1 for 21.

Super Bowl XIII between Dallas and Pittsburgh was not only the highest-scoring game in the series but probably the best.

DORSETT
STAUBACH

Above: *Steeler Franco Harris (32) makes his 18-yard dash to Pittsburgh's fourth TD.*

Left: *Dallas' Roger Staubach (12) looks for a receiver. He passed for 228 and three TDs, an outstanding performance – but Bradshaw's was even better.*

Right: *Steeler Terry Bradshaw, sacked by LB Tom Henderson.*

The thirteenth edition of the Super Bowl rescued the event, albeit briefly, from its growing reputation as an unfulfilling exercise in hype. For the first time in several years, the NFL championship offered a match of classic teams: the Pittsburgh Steelers versus the Dallas Cowboys. Each had won the Super Bowl twice before. Each franchise had captured the imagination of fans across the country. At stake was the claim of being the decade's dominant team.

The power image from Pittsburgh was its Steel Curtain defense, which gave up a league-low 195 points as the Steelers shoved their way to a 14-2 record. On offense, quarterback Terry Bradshaw had attracted his share of criticism, but he finished the regular season with nearly 3000 yards passing and a league-high 28 touchdown passes (he also threw 20 interceptions). And Franco Harris had another 1000-yard season rushing. If any questions remained about the team's legitimacy, most of them were answered in the AFC championship game when the Steelers drilled the Houston Oilers, 34-5.

The Cowboys, on the other hand, frittered away the early season, piled up a 6-4 record and did little to instill confidence that they could regroup. Then, just as folks in Texas were bordering on disgust, the Pokes won their last six games, including a key 37-10 smashing of Washington in a Thanksgiving Day showdown. From there, they rolled on, flattening the Rams, 28-0, in the NFC championship game. Only one question remained from the 1978 season, and it would be answered in Miami's Orange Bowl. Sort of. Refreshingly, this was a game where anticipation and actuality met on the same plane. 'Finally,' William N Wallace wrote in the *New York Times*, 'a Super Bowl.'

Despite their status as defending world champions, the Cowboys were underdogs. 'We're the challengers, even though we've got the championship,' conceded Cowboys defensive end Harvey Martin. Martin and the other members of the Dallas defensive front – tackle Randy White, end Ed 'Too Tall' Jones, Larry Cole, Jethro Pugh and Larry Stalls – would take on Pittsburgh's efficient offensive line, including Kolb, all-pro center Mike Webster, Ray Pinney and Gerry Mullins.

From their early press comments, the two units seemed to be mutual admiration societies. 'Kolb, in my eyes,' Martin told reporters, 'is the best executing offensive tackle in football. He's not the biggest, and I don't think he's really the strongest, like a lot of people say. But he is the best lineman they have, and I know Webster is all-pro and their whole line is one of the best executing in the league.'

'Harvey is probably the best,' Kolb said in return. That congeniality, however, didn't extend to other positions. Dallas free safety Cliff Harris readily talked to reporters of how he planned to hit Steeler receiver Lynn Swann hard, 'not to hurt him, but that doesn't mean he might not get hurt.'

And if that didn't make things hot enough, Thomas 'Hollywood' Henderson, the Cowboys' outrageous linebacker, stirred the coals a bit by announcing to the press that Pittsburgh quarterback Terry Bradshaw was so dumb he couldn't spell 'cat' if you spotted him the 'c' and the 'a.' Bradshaw's response? Merely 318 yards and four touchdowns passing (both Super Bowl records at that time) and the game's MVP trophy as the Steelers won, 35-31. The victory made them the first team in NFL history to win three Super Bowls (they would add a fourth the following year against the Los Angeles Rams).

Afterwards, Bradshaw basked in the locker room with a smile and told reporters, 'Go ask Henderson if I was dumb today.'

The game wasn't a masterpiece, rather a collector's item, a somewhat jazzed up reprint of Pittsburgh's 21-17 victory over the Cowboys in Super Bowl X. Having beaten Denver soundly in Super Bowl XII, the Cowboys had seemed confident the outcome of their rematch with Pittsburgh would be otherwise.

Dallas took the opening kickoff and moved to two quick first downs and excellent field position at the Pittsburgh 35. There Drew Pearson fumbled on a double reverse/pass option, and the Steelers recovered at their 47. Moments later, Bradshaw hit John Stallworth with the first of his touchdown passes for a 7-0 lead. The Steeler defense then seemed to have things under control until Bradshaw was sacked toward the end of the first quarter (the Dallas defense would sack him four times over the afternoon) and fumbled in his own territory. Roger Staubach quickly cashed in the gift certificate with a 39-yard scoring pass to Tony Hill.

Then in the second quarter, the Dallas defense declared doomsday again, as Henderson and fellow

Top: *Steeler Lynn Swann with WR John Stallworth (82) and RB Franco Harris (32).*

Above: *Dallas coach Tom Landry.*

Right: *Linebacker Mike Hegman scored Dallas' second TD after he recovered a Bradshaw fumble and ran it 37 yards.*

linebacker Mike Hegman sacked Bradshaw and stripped him of the ball. Hegman did the honors, running in for the score from 37 yards out to give Dallas a 14-7 edge. Stallworth erased that minutes later when he pulled in a Bradshaw pass at the Pittsburgh 35, shook the tackle of safety Aaron Kyle and sprinted to the end zone, turning a routine pattern into a 75-yard score. Things continued to sour for the Cowboys on the following possession as Staubach threw an interception to Mel Blount. Bradshaw threw a seven-yarder to Rocky Bleier just before the half for a 21-14 Steeler lead.

In the third the Dallas downslide continued. Jackie Smith, the former St Louis Cardinal tight end who had come out of retirement to bolster the Cowboys' lineup, was open in the end zone but slipped, and the tying touchdown pass bounced off his shoulder pad. 'I was wide open and I missed it,' said a dejected Smith. Dallas kicked a field goal on the next play and trailed, 21-17, going into the fourth.

Then the downslide became an avalanche, and the rumble that started it all was a pass interference call against Dallas, a controversy that will steam in Dallas for decades. Cowboy defensive back Benny Barnes and Swann collided on an alley oop pass play that gave Pittsburgh a first down at the Dallas 23. Moments later Franco Harris scored on a 22-yard run to give the Steelers a 28-17 lead.

'I was tripped once and tripped again,' Swann told reporters afterwards. 'I didn't push off. And when I fell that wasn't an act on my part. There was no act involved. I was trying to get to the ball, because if I get to the ball, it's six points.' Barnes, however, complained that Swann had pushed him. 'I felt the shove, and I went down,' the Cowboys' cornerback said. 'The ref called it tripping. That's what he called. The refs are right. The game's over. The officials are human, but this was absurd. Maybe he needs glasses or maybe he's from Pittsburgh, I don't know.'

'It was a judgment call on a pass play,' Fred Swearingen, the field judge said. 'The two players bumped before the ball was thrown. They were both looking back, and the defender went to the ground. The Pittsburgh receiver, in trying to get to the ball, was tripped by the defender's feet. The receiver was trying to get to the ball. It was coming to him in that direction, and I threw the flag for pass interference.'

Dallas coach Tom Landry was obviously disturbed: 'If they called it for pushing, it was a good call. If not, it was a bad call. When they throw that kind of an alley-oop pass, body contact is nothing. There's always body contact. It's a crazy pass, and they got the yardage out of it, that's what bothers me.' Indeed, if the call had gone against Swann for offensive interference, the Steelers would have faced third and 20 at their own 29.

As it was, just 14 seconds after the call, the Cowboys were struck by the second quake. Randy White, who played on the kick return team, fumbled a short kickoff. Pittsburgh recovered, and Bradshaw threw 18 yards to Lynn Swann for a 35-17 lead with a little over six minutes left.

On the Steeler sidelines, the celebration began. Bradshaw saw Staubach trot onto the field and reminded his teammates that it was too early. Sure enough, the Cowboys drove 89 yards and scored to make it 35-24 with 2:27 left. Then they recovered the onsides kick, and eight plays later, Staubach hit Butch Johnson with a four-yard pass for a 35-31 score with 0:22 on the clock. This time, however, Bleier covered the onsides kick, and Pittsburgh coach Chuck Noll had his third Super Bowl trophy.

'They played their hearts out,' Tom said of his players.

The outcome left Franco Harris, who gained 68 yards on 20 carries, with the feeling that he had been part of one of football's special moments. 'The Steelers and the Cowboys have played the two most exciting games ever in the Super Bowl,' he said. 'I give credit to Dallas because they didn't quit. They kept our defense out there in the fourth quarter. They really gave us a scare.'

For the Steelers, the passing game was the obvious difference. Staubach had thrown for 228 yards for Dallas. But Bradshaw had made the big plays. 'Our plan was to throw to the wide receivers,' Swann said.

'That way the Dallas cornerbacks would have to come up and make the tackles, and the cornerbacks aren't as good at tackling as the two safeties.' As things turned out, it was a pretty good plan.

Early in the game, Cliff Harris had hammered Swann just as he had indicated he would earlier in the week. 'That was a good clean shot in the chest,' Swann said of the hit. 'But as for the talk during the week, I'm at the point where in my mind I could blast every player on the Cowboys who talked about me, but I prefer to take the position I normally take and let the result speak for itself.' Swann didn't deny that the interference call was crucial: 'If we don't get the touchdown there (on the pass interference call), who knows?' he said. 'And if we only get a field goal there, that's three points instead of seven points – a four-point difference. And as it turned out, with the way the Cowboys came back at the end, those four points were the difference in the score.'

In the Dallas locker room, Hollywood Henderson had difficulty holding back the tears of disappointment. As for Bradshaw, he had a new three-letter word to spell: W-I-N.

Left: *Bradshaw passed for 318 and four TDs on 17 completions.*

Above: *Pittsburgh coach Chuck Noll with Bradshaw.*

Below: *By game's end Steeler Franco Harris (32) was the Super Bowl's leading rusher, having gained 308 yards in the course of three games.*

Super Bowl XIV

Pittsburgh Steelers 31, Los Angeles Rams 19

20 January 1980
Rose Bowl, Pasadena, Calif.
Attendance: 103,985

Los Angeles	7	6	6	0	—	19
Pittsburgh	3	7	7	14	—	31

Pittsburgh – Field goal, 41, Bahr.
Los Angeles – Bryant, 1, run (Corral kick).
Pittsburgh – Harris, 1, run (Bahr kick).
Los Angeles – Field goal, 31, Corral.
Los Angeles – Field goal, 45, Corral.
Pittsburgh – Swann, 47, pass from Bradshaw (Bahr kick).
Los Angeles – R. Smith, 24, pass from McCutcheon (kick failed).
Pittsburgh – Stallworth, 73, pass from Bradshaw (Bahr kick).
Pittsburgh – Harris, 1, run (Bahr kick).

Rushing: *Los Angeles* – Tyler, 17 for 60; Bryant, 6 for 30, 1 TD; McCutcheon, 5 for 10; Ferragamo, 1 for 7. *Pittsburgh* – Harris, 20 for 46, 2 TD; Bleier, 10 for 25; Bradshaw, 3 for 9; Thornton, 4 for 4.
Passing: *Los Angeles* – Ferragamo, 15 of 25 for 212, 1 int; McCutcheon, 1 of 1 for 24, 1 TD. *Pittsburgh* – Bradshaw, 14 of 21 for 309, 2 TD, 3 int.
Receiving: *Los Angeles* – Waddy, 3 for 75; Bryant, 3 for 21; Tyler, 3 for 20; Dennard, 2 for 32; Nelson, 2 for 20; D Hill, 1 for 28; Smith, 1 for 24, 1 TD; McCutcheon, 1 for 16. *Pittsburgh* – Swann, 5 for 79, 1 TD; Stallworth, 3 for 121, 1 TD; Harris, 3 for 66; Cunningham, 2 for 21; Thornton, 1 for 22.
Punting: *Los Angeles* – Clark, 5 for 44.0 average. *Pittsburgh* – Colquitt, 2 for 42.5.
Punt Returns: *Los Angeles* – Brown, 1 for 4. *Pittsburgh* – Bell, 2 for 17; Smith, 2 for 14.
Kickoff Returns: *Los Angeles* – E Hill, 3 for 47; Jodat, 2 for 32; Andrews, 1 for 0. *Pittsburgh* – L Anderson, 5 for 162.
Interceptions: *Los Angeles* – Elmendorf, 1 for 10; Brown, 1 for 6; Perry, 1 for –1; Thomas, 0 for 6. *Pittsburgh* – Lambert, 1 for 16.

Super Bowl XIV. Ram RB Cullen Bryant (32) has just bulled over from the one to score Los Angeles' first Super Bowl TD.

77
47
29
58

Success has sometimes followed strange paths in pro football, but seldom more so than for the Los Angeles Rams in 1979. Their final destination turned out to be a mere footnote in football history. They were the eventual losers in Super Bowl XIV, where the Pittsburgh Steelers won an unprecedented fourth Super Bowl title. But probably no Super Bowl loser has gotten more satisfaction out of the close to a season.

In mid-November 1979, the Rams' roster was decimated by injuries, a factor reflected by their 5-6 record in the NFC's weak Western Division. Along with running back John Capaletti, their corps of receivers and defensive backs was the hardest hit. Then quarterback Pat Haden broke his finger, bringing on Vince Ferragamo as the replacement. Despite his lack of experience, Ferragamo had a strong arm and soon proved that he could fill in adequately. LA coach Ray Malavasi relied heavily on his running game featuring backs Wendell Tyler and Cullen Bryant. With three victories in the final four games, Ferragamo led the Rams into the playoffs against the Dallas Cowboys, who had reached the postseason with an 11-5 record.

Down 14-5 at the half, the Cowboys took a 19-14 lead in the fourth quarter and appeared headed to the next round until Ferragamo connected with wide receiver Billy Waddy on a 50-yard touchdown pass. LA won, 21-19. Ferragamo completed only nine of 21

Above: *The Pittsburgh defense dumps Ram Wendell Tyler (26).*

Left: *Ram QB Vince Ferragamo.*

Right: *Steeler WR Lynn Swann (88) goes down. On the day, Swann caught five for 79 yards and one TD (on a 75-yard pass from Terry Bradshaw).*

passing attempts, but three went for touchdowns.

For six straight years, the Rams had failed in the playoffs, leaving their fans stranded among false hopes often enough that the team had few true believers in 1979. In the NFC championship game against the upstart Tampa Bay Buccaneers, Ferragamo threw no touchdown passes. As expected, the game was a defensive standoff, and perhaps Ferragamo was the difference. He completed 12 of 23 passes for 163 yards and no interceptions, just enough to drive the Rams to three field goals. Kicker Frank

Corral was true on all three, and Los Angeles was headed to Super Bowl XIV at the Rose Bowl in nearby Pasadena.

In the American Conference, the Steelers moved into the playoffs on what could best be described as an all-out year by Terry Bradshaw. With three Super Bowl titles under his belt, he seemed willing to take chances. Sometimes they worked. He passed for 3724 yards and 26 touchdown passes. But he also threw 25 interceptions, as the Steelers finished 12-4. Harris again was the force in the running game with 1186 yards rushing.

In the playoffs, coach Chuck Noll's boys made quick work of the Dolphins by scoring 20 points in the first quarter, including two TD passes from Bradshaw, on their way to a 30-14 rout.

The AFC championship game brought a brief scare when Houston's Vernon Perry picked off a Bradshaw pass on the sixth play of the game and raced 75 yards for a score to give the Oilers a 7-0 lead. But the Steeler defense shut down the running of Houston's Earl Campbell, and Bradshaw came back to throw two touchdown passes as Pittsburgh won, 27-13, and headed back to the Super Bowl for a shot at an unprecedented fourth title.

The Rams were just elated to be in their company. Still, there was no great excitement among Los Angeles followers, at least not in the opinion of Wendell Tyler, who described them as 'weekly fans, not dedicated fans, not like in the East – you can go out before the game and get booed.'

The Steelers were the dominant team of the seventies about to stamp their brand on the first few days of the eighties. They had a proud tradition in playoff games over the decade, a 13-4 record including a 3-0 tally in Super Bowls. 'Our coach says when you lose, say little,' said Pittsburgh defensive tackle Steve Furness, 'and when you win, say nothing.'

Yet there was a chink in the Steelers' black-and-gold armor. They had not beaten the Rams since 1956, and in fact, had only beaten Los Angeles once in the long history of the two franchises (a 1-12-1 record against the Rams). 'I've never played well against them,' Terry Bradshaw told reporters. His record against the Rams was 0-3. Fortunately, the Pittsburgh offense was far from one dimensional with running back Franco Harris and wide receivers Lynn Swann and John Stallworth. But the real significance of the won-loss statistics in recent years involved the coaching. Three of Noll's assistants in Pittsburgh – defensive coordinator Bud Carson, receiver coach Lionel Taylor and offensive line coach Dan Radakovich – had been hired away by the Rams. Noll sought to minimize that factor, saying, 'It's a trade-off. They know us, but we know them.'

But Carson was proud of the Rams' success against

Left: *Pittsburgh's QB, Terry Bradshaw, fades back to pass behind a wall of blockers. No 57 is guard Sam Davis, 52 is center Mike Webster and 79 is tackle Larry Brown. Bradshaw, the game's MVP, threw for an extraordinary 309 yards.*

Right: *Steeler wide receiver John Stallworth, too, had a good day, catching three for 121. His most spectacular play came in the last quarter, when he caught a 39-yard Bradshaw pass and ran it 34 more yards for a 73-yard touchdown.*

the Steelers, particularly in their 10-7 victory during the 1978 season. 'We played a little differently that night,' Carson said. 'We used some pass coverages they weren't used to.'

But the defensive coach also pointed out it would be very difficult to control Stallworth and Swann, Pittsburgh's excellent receivers. 'We've only got 11 players,' he said. 'We can't double those two great wide receivers on every play, so there has to be times when one of the cornerbacks won't have any help. But another key is first down. If we can stop them on first down we've got a chance.'

The Steeler passing game was hard to defend against because the running game worked so well. The Pittsburgh offense never seemed to be in an obvious passing situation. 'In an obvious passing situation,' Carson, who directed Pittsburgh's Steel Curtain defense for six years until leaving the club in 1978, told reporters, 'we can get a fifth defensive back in there who will give us double coverage on both wide receivers. And against Bradshaw, you need that. I think Bradshaw is the best quarterback there is. Nobody has an arm like he has. And if he's running around, he's hard to bring down. He shades off linebackers. He doesn't always scramble for yardage. He mostly buys time to throw. But he's likely to run a lot more in a Super Bowl game because the season is all over. They'll turn him loose.'

As the former receiver coach of the Steelers, Lionel Taylor knew the inside scoop on the Pittsburgh air game. 'For this game,' he told reporters, 'the thing I've tried to impress on my receivers is, each second expect to get hit because the Steelers hit people hard. But our defensive backs have been asking me about Swann and Stallworth, who I had for four seasons. I just remind them how high Swann can leap and that Stallworth is tough to bring down. You can't one-arm him.'

As with most linemen, offensive line coach Radakovich thought the game would be won in the trenches. 'We've got to move the ball,' he said, 'and we've got to make four or five big plays.' That seemed to be a substantial challenge. Led by linebacker Jack Lambert, the Steeler defense had shut down the best running games in the league. Earl Campbell, known far and wide for his brutal running style, had gained

Left: *Los Angeles cornerback Pat Thomas looks as though he were about to hurl Lynn Swann out of the Rose Bowl. The Rams mounted a good defense on the ground, but they could not handle the Steelers' aerial offensive.*

15 yards in 17 attempts against the Steelers in the AFC championship.

Still, the Rams were brimming with new-found confidence. 'We can run on anyone,' declared Doug France, the left tackle. And the LA offensive line was no slouch at pass blocking, either. 'We timed the films of one play in the Tampa game,' said Pittsburgh's Steve Furness, 'and Ferragamo had eight and a half seconds to pass. He looked both ways, dropped his hands to his sides, then pump-faked and looked off another guy before throwing.' Still, the analysts doubted Ferragamo's ability to challenge Pittsburgh. In his limited playing time during the regular season, he completed 48 percent of his passes and threw 10 interceptions against only five TD passes. But his performance in Super Bowl XIV would reflect little of that. Rather, he was confident, even gutsy, connecting on 15 of 25 attempts for 212 yards, enough to push LA to a surprising 19-17 third-quarter lead.

'We didn't expect them to roll over dead,' Pittsburgh tight end Bennie Cunningham said later, 'but we probably didn't think it would be as difficult as it turned out to be in the game.'

'I wasn't surprised at the way the Rams played,' said Joe Greene, the Steelers' all-pro tackle. 'They believed they could win. That's what makes great teams.'

'Things were not going the way we would have liked them to go,' Stallworth said. 'We needed the big play.' The only problem was, half the Steelers' big-play offense went down in the third quarter when Lynn Swann left with an injury. The Steelers, however, gained their footing early in the fourth quarter and found the necessary touchdown when Stallworth turned a routine pass play into a footrace to the goal line. Stallworth got a step on cornerback Rod Perry, and when safety Eddie Brown failed to help out, the Pittsburgh receiver beat the LA secondary, giving Pittsburgh a 24-19 lead.

'That's something I don't do,' Brown said. 'I don't make mistakes. I did tonight. They'll blame Rod, but I should have been there. I would have had at least a play on it.'

'If I could have made a big play, tipped the ball away, I think I could have turned the tides a little bit,' Perry said.

'Terry threw the ball deep enough away from Perry that he couldn't make a play,' Stallworth said. 'There was a hand right in there at the last second that almost tipped it. I was lucky it didn't break my concentration.'

Ferragamo immediately turned the Rams around and headed them downfield to the Pittsburgh 32. There he made his only mistake of the day, throwing a pass that was picked off by Steeler linebacker Jack Lambert. Afterward, Ferragamo conceded he should have looked for another option. 'We were in reverse coverage,' said Lambert. 'We worked against that play all week. And the ball came where we expected it. I don't think Ferragamo ever saw me.'

On Pittsburgh's ensuing drive, a pass interference call helped move the ball into scoring position, and Franco killed off LA's hopes with a one-yard plunge for a 31-19 lead, the final margin. Rams coach Ray Malavasi complained about the crucial penalty. 'It was a bad call,' he said. Charlie Musser, the field

judge who made the call, defended his judgment: 'The defender had good position all the way on the play until the last second, when he played the man instead of the ball.'

On the day, Bradshaw completed 14 of 21 for 309 yards and two touchdowns, but he also threw three interceptions. Still, the numbers made him the top vote getter for the MVP Award. Ferragamo, who had entered the game with the analysts doubting his abilities, rose to the occasion. The Super Bowl had shown what a fine quarterback Ferragamo was.

'They didn't outplay us,' said Malavasi. 'We ran on them, we threw on them, we just didn't get the big plays. I thought we were going to win right from the beginning and I thought so right to the end.'

'I thought everybody played well,' commented Ferragamo. 'We just weren't good enough to win.'

Injured late in the regular season, the Steelers' all-pro linebacker, Jack Ham, watched the game from the sidelines. He was impressed by what he saw. 'We can grind it out or make the big plays,' he said. 'I thought Jack Lambert played a great game at middle linebacker. The Rams played as well as they could have. We didn't play well for the whole game, but we played well enough to win. It was a big-play game, and today we came up with more big plays than they did.' Ham had it about right.

Opposite left: *The Rams' young Vince Ferragamo did a great job at QB – better, some said, even than Bradshaw.*

Opposite right: *By the end of the game Franco Harris' Super Bowl rushing total had climbed to 354 yards.*

Left: *Despite the efforts of Ram CB Rod Perry, Stallworth will catch this TD pass over his shoulder.*

Top: *The Steelers' 260-lb DT 'Mean' Joe Greene symbolized the Pittsburgh defense.*

Above: *Rams coach Ray Malvasi.*

Super Bowl XV

Oakland Raiders 27, Philadelphia Eagles 10

25 January 1981
Louisiana Superdome, New Orleans
Attendance: 76,135

Oakland	14	0	10	3	—	27
Philadelphia	0	3	0	7	—	10

Oakland – Branch, 2, pass from Plunkett (Bahr kick).
Oakland – King, 80, pass from Plunkett (Bahr kick).
Philadelphia – Field goal, 30, Franklin.
Oakland – Branch, 29, pass from Plunkett (Bahr kick).
Oakland – Field goal, 46, Bahr.
Philadelphia – Krepfle, 8, pass from Jaworski (Franklin kick).
Oakland – Field goal, 35, Bahr.

Rushing: *Oakland* – van Eeghen, 19 for 80; King, 6 for 18; Jensen, 3 for 12; Plunkett, 3 for 9; Whittington, 3 for –2. *Philadelphia* – Montgomery, 16 for 44; Harris, 7 for 14; Giamonna, 1 for 7; Harrington, 1 for 4; Jaworski, 1 for 0.
Passing: *Oakland* – Plunkett, 13 of 21 for 261, 3 TD. *Philadelphia* – Jaworski, 18 of 38 for 291, 1 TD, 3 int.
Receiving: *Oakland* – Branch, 5 for 67, 2 TD; Chandler, 4 for 77; King, 2 for 93, 1 TD; Chester, 2 for 24. *Philadelphia* – Montgomery, 6 for 91; Carmichael, 5 for 83, Smith, 2 for 59; Krepfle, 2 for 16, 1 TD; Spagnola, 1 for 22; Parker, 1 for 19; Harris, 1 for 1.
Punting: *Oakland* – Guy, 3 for 42.0 average. *Philadelphia* – Runager, 3 for 36.7.
Punt Returns: *Oakland* – Matthews, 2 for 1. *Philadelphia* – Sciarra, 2 for 18; Henry, 1 for 2.
Kickoff Returns: *Oakland* – Matthews, 2 for 29; Moody, 1 for 19. *Philadelphia* – Campfield, 5 for 87; Harrington, 1 for 0.
Interceptions: *Oakland* – Martin, 3 for 44. *Philadelphia* – None.

Super Bowl XV. Linebacker Rod Martin (53) intercepted three Eagle passes, for a Raider gain of 44 yards.

Two aging quarterbacks came face to face in Super Bowl XV after struggling through years of unfulfilled promise. And as quarterbacks will do, one had a great day, the other wretched time, in the Louisiana Super Bowl. Regardless of the outcome, both had salvaged more than a bit of respect for their careers from the 1980 season.

Just as the Philadelphia Eagles had emerged suddenly from the NFL pack to usher in the 1960s, they made an abrupt appearance in the 1980 Super Bowl, moving mostly on the wits of coach Dick Vermeil and the arm of veteran quarterback Ron Jaworksi. Unlike their 1960 edition, the Eagles failed to win the championship. That, of course, would fall to the Oakland Raiders, the first wild-card team to win its way to the Vince Lombardi Trophy in the 15-year life of the Super Bowl.

The season had brought a changed look to the Raiders. Ken Stabler had been traded for Dan Pastorini, and coach John Madden had retired to become a CBS TV analyst, giving the reins over to his assistant, Tom Flores.

The year, however, belonged to Oakland backup quarterback, Jim Plunkett, the Heisman winner out of Stanford who had won AFC Rookie of the Year honors in 1971 with New England, then drifted into anonymity. He would have remained there if Pastorini hadn't suffered a fractured leg in a loss to Kansas City the fifth game of the season. Plunkett took over from there, driving the Raiders to an 11-5 record and a wild-card spot in the playoffs. There they hammered Houston, 27-7, then eased by Brian Sipe and Cleveland, 14-12, and played a grand game against favored San Diego and Dan Fouts for the AFC title.

The newspaper coverage of the season became a testimonial to the perseverance of Plunkett's career. 'Jim Plunkett is the most efficient quarterback I've ever played with,' Cliff Branch, the Raiders' wide receiver, told reporters. 'He can take off and scramble, and that gives us a lot of sting. Kenny could get the ball deep, but the key to stopping Stabler is putting pressure on him, because he can't maneuver. Plunkett can scramble. Plunkett has been the leader we didn't have when Dan was in there. Dan didn't know the Raiders' system, but Plunkett knew it.'

With Plunkett's passing and the running of Kenny King and Mark van Eeghen, the Raiders ran out to a 28-7 first-half lead. Fouts finally jumpstarted his offensive machine, but the Oakland defense, led by Ted Hendricks, Lester Hayes and John Matuszak, held on for a 34-27 win.

Over in the NFC, the proceedings were as confusing as usual. The sports world had figured the Dallas Cowboys might be Oakland's Super Bowl opponent after Tom Landry's team had whipped the Eagles badly at the close of the regular season. But the Eagles made a comeback in their last regular-season game and won the Eastern Division crown, finishing the schedule 12-4.

It had been a fine year for Ron Jaworski, who completed 57 percent of his passing attempts for 3529 yards and 27 touchdowns with only 12 interceptions. He had come out of Youngstown State in the 1973

Left: *The scene of SB XV was the Louisiana Superdome in New Orleans.*

Left below: *Oakland LB Ted Hendricks (83) blocks an Eagle field goal attempt.*

Right: *The game was something of a personal vindication for the Raiders' veteran QB, Jim Plunkett. 'All Jim needed was for someone to believe in him,' said coach Tom Flores after Oakland's big win.*

NFL draft and found a spot as a backup quarterback with the Los Angeles Rams. Then in 1977 he was traded to the Eagles, where he teamed with Vermeil to bring the franchise some of its best years. In 1978 Jaworski drove the Eagles to a 9-7 record and a wild-card playoff spot. Their Super Bowl hopes had ended early, when Atlanta beat them, 14-13, in the first round. The next year, Jaworski and the Eagles ran their record to 11-5, good for another wild-card shot. But that, too, was ended early, 24-17, by Tampa Bay.

Much of Jaworski's reputation around the league rested with his rocket arm. 'When I was growing up I was a catcher,' he said. 'I used to throw from a crouch position all arm. I didn't use my body to throw the ball. I don't think anyone has my velocity. I've got another thing I do different. I have my wrist cocked when my arm's back here,' he said, demonstrating his technique. 'Most people have their wrist locked and then open it when it's here. Mine is ready to go.'

Other observers credited the success of the Eagle passing game to Sid Gillman, the former San Diego coach and passing innovator who branded his stamp on the early AFL. 'I don't want to discuss what my contribution has been,' Gillman said, directing the attention instead to Jaworski. 'If I were going into a new franchise, I'd take him right quick.'

Vermeil, of course, had done just that. 'I love Ron Jaworski,' he said. 'He's the Lackawanna guy (a reference to Jaworski's small hometown in New York), that's why I like him. I spend a lot of time with him. I spend as much time with my players as anybody in pro football.'

All that mutual admiration and work seemed for naught early in the opening round of the playoffs when the Minnesota Vikings jumped out to a 14-0 lead over the Eagles. Then Philadelphia running back Wilbert Montgomery scored two touchdowns, and the Eagles' young defense tightened. The Eagles scored the final 17 points of the game to win going away, 31-16.

The NFC championship game against Dallas figured to be a tough one. It was, but in the chill of Philadelphia's Veterans Stadium, running back Wilbert Montgomery chugged his way to 194 yards rushing. The defense, led by end Carl Hairston, shut down Dallas in the second half, and the Eagles won, 20-7.

With Philadelphia and Oakland meeting in the Super Bowl in New Orleans, the media immediately focused on the image of the owners and their teams. Oakland's Al Davis and NFL Commissioner Pete Rozelle were known for their dislike of each other. Rozelle had once called Davis 'an outlaw,' an image that the press seized because it suited his Raiders so well. Davis, his staff and his players had cultivated that idea to a good degree and they used his apparent clash with Rozelle as a motivational factor. It seemed to give them strength. The rest of the league, of course, sought to downplay that. 'People are being made to believe there is a personal vendetta between Commissioner Rozelle and Al Davis,' Bears owner George Halas said. 'This is totally false. Commissioner Rozelle speaks for 28 franchises known as the National Football League. His voice protects them. Commissioner Rozelle is as concerned about Al Davis and the future of the Oakland Raiders as he is about George Halas and the future of the Chicago Bears.'

There were suggestions that the Raiders' black-and-silver image as the Darth Vaders of football was a bit overworked. 'People put things in images these days,' John Madden said. 'When the Eagles picked up

7

Left: *Eagle QB Ron Jaworski was, like Plunkett, a veteran making a come-back. This game would disappoint his hopes.*

Right: *Philadelphia coach Dick Vermeil with Pete Rozelle.*

Claude Humphrey, he was Eagleized, he was Dick Vermellized. But if the Raiders had picked up Claude Humphrey, he would have been another renegade, another of Al's reclamation projects.'

Over the years, Davis had built his team and his reputation on the unique gambles he took on players, both young, untested ones and older ones whose careers had gone awry. Plunkett was an example of the latter. Cornerback Lester Hayes, a fifth-round draft pick out of Texas A&M who stammered badly, was one of Davis' young gambles. 'You have to judge the intelligence of those who thought that Lester was too dumb,' Davis once remarked. 'I never believe in the cliche that a player is too dumb. I think we've got to be smart enough to teach him how to play.'

The Super Bowl appearance by his wild-card team once again offered reinforcement of Davis and his Raiders, right down to their 'outlaw' image. But even Davis didn't want that image going too far. 'When the Chicago Bears were the Monsters of the Midway, they wore black,' he told reporters. 'And when Army had those great teams, they wore black – the Black Knights of the Hudson.'

Philadelphia owner Leonard Tose was a study in contrasts, an owner as cooperative with Rozelle and the league as Davis was confrontational. 'Al loves to create controversy,' Tose told reporters in the days before the game, 'and I try to avoid it.' While Davis had a reputation for remaining involved in his coaches' game plans, Tose was a hands-off owner. 'I don't know anything about football,' he said modestly. 'I'd only be an interference.'

The on-field strategy seemed to take a back seat to the hype. Flores had great confidence in his Raiders despite their wild-card status. 'We don't have a good percentage of pass completions,' he said, 'but we're a big play team. We are able to go deep, not only to our wide receivers, but to our running backs.' That confidence was felt among the Raider veterans as well. 'I kept reminding our players during the playoffs that the only thing winning does is it lets you play the next week,' offensive guard Gene Upshaw said. 'But unless you win the Super Bowl, everything else is down. You can remember the Steelers won four Super Bowls, but you never remember who they beat. When you come here for the first time, you tend to be happy just being here. But until you win the Super Bowl, you haven't won anything. That's the difference. That's what experience will do.'

As for Jaworski, he had the Raider defense to ponder. 'If we get into second and third down we'll be in trouble against Oakland,' he predicted all too accurately. 'They bring in the extra defensive back and an extra down lineman and they give Ted Hendricks freedom to do what he wants to do.'

In the Louisiana Superdome, Jaworski completed 18 of 38 attempts for 291 yards and a touchdown. But he was rushed hard by the Oakland defensive line and threw three interceptions, all of them to Raider defensive back Rod Martin. The three interceptions by one player was a Super Bowl record, one of six different records set on the day.

Plunkett and the Raiders quickly established who had the magic, as he threw two first quarter touchdowns, confirming Flores' notions about the big play. Philadelphia answered only with a second quarter field goal and trailed, 14-3, at the half. Plunkett opened the third quarter with his third TD pass, the second of the day to Cliff Branch. On the day, the Oakland quarterback completed 13 of 21 passes for 261 yards and three touchdowns to win the MVP honors and the game, 27-10. A second award should have gone to his offensive line. 'We made up our minds they weren't going to touch Jim,' veteran lineman Art Shell commented afterward.

'I can't say enough about him,' Flores said of Plunkett to the locker room crowd of reporters. 'He met every challenge this season with style and class. He has great competitive spirit and deserves all the credit in the world.'

Plunkett basked in the crowd of reporters around him afterward. 'I started the day so pumped up that I was exhausted before the end of the pre-game warm-ups,' he said. 'It may not look like it and it may not sound like it, but I'm going through a tremendous state of euphoria. It's something that I've often dreamt about, but I never thought I would be standing here giving this type of interview. This is my greatest moment as a professional. This is certainly the best club I've ever played with. . . . The game plan was to look for the opportunity to go for the big play. On the first touchdown, everyone was covered and as I started to run, the defenders left Cliff and came toward me, leaving him open. On the second one, I wanted to hit Bob Chandler but he was covered so I scrambled to my left and saw Kenny waving his arms. I just threw the ball as hard as I could, trying to get it by the defender or hard enough so he couldn't intercept it. Cliff (Branch) made just a spectacular play on the third one. It was simply a tremendous effort. I saw him open and let go and I didn't expect the defensive back to move into the area. Cliff just went right around him and made a great play.'

Branch, who caught five passes for 67 yards and two TDs, said, 'I think Plunkett is a hell of an athlete and he deserves to be where he is today. The play wasn't designed to go deep – I was supposed to go six yards and stop but when I saw him start to scramble I kept going. It's amazing how a guy could get that much on the ball moving to his left and almost away from the receiver. It takes a great athlete.'

The Raider defense had performed in step with the offense. 'I studied and studied all week,' Rod Martin said of his record-setting three interceptions. 'I sat in my bed after curfew and looked at film.'

For Philadelphia, the search for consolation was a struggle. 'I am most disappointed we let our fans down,' said Tose. 'We got here, but we didn't take advantage of the opportunity we had. It just didn't look like the Eagles I know. You should always be remembered, in part, for what you did in the Super Bowl. I would think it will leave a bad taste in my mouth.'

'I just didn't feel like we got into the flow of the game,' Jaworski said. 'I felt we had great practices and we'd come out smoking. We didn't.'

Words of consolation came from a backup quarterback. 'Ron Jaworski brought us here,' said Joe Pisarcik. 'Nobody can sit back and criticize him. We won together and we lost together.'

With their second Super Bowl title in a half decade, the Raiders were left to revel in their image. 'We weren't going to pull any horns back,' Flores said. 'We were going to go with the big play. We were going to go after them. And it just worked out fine.'

'It was the world against us,' Upshaw added. 'And everybody said we didn't have a chance. They kept reminding us we're not supposed to win. If we played again next week, we'd be picked to lose.'

Opposite top: *Jim Plunkett, who passed for 261 and three TDs, was the game's MVP.*

Opposite below: *Two Oakland scores were made by WR Cliff Branch, here engaged in some fancy receiver's balletics.*

Above: *Another outstanding Raider was kicker Chris Bahr, who made two field goals and three extra points.*

Left: *Raider LB Jeff Barnes signals the end of an Eagle drive while TE John Spagnola looks on glumly.*

Super Bowl XVI

San Francisco 49ers 26, Cincinnati Bengals 21

24 January 1982
Pontiac (Mich.) Silverdome
Attendance: 81,270

San Francisco	7	13	0	6	—	26
Cincinnati	0	0	7	14	—	21

San Francisco– Montana, 1, run (Wersching kick).
San Francisco – Cooper, 11, pass from Montana (Wersching kick).
San Francisco – Field goal, 22, Wersching.
San Francisco – Field goal, 26, Wersching.
Cincinnati – Anderson, 5, run (Breech kick).
Cincinnati – Ross, 4, pass from Anderson (Breech kick).
San Francisco – Field goal, 40, Wersching.
San Francisco – Field goal, 23, Wersching.
Cincinnati – Ross, 3, pass from Anderson (Breech kick).

Rushing: *San Francisco* – Patton, 17 for 55; Cooper, 9 for 34; Montana, 6 for 18, 1 TD; Ring, 5 for 17; Davis, 2 for 5; Clark, 1 for –2. *Cincinnati* – Johnson, 14 for 36; Alexander, 5 for 17; Anderson, 4 for 15, 1 TD; A Griffin, 1 for 4.
Passing: *San Francisco* – Montana, 14 of 22 for 157, 1 TD. *Cincinnati* – Anderson, 25 of 34 for 300, 2 TD, 2 int.
Receiving: *San Francisco* – Solomon, 4 for 52; Clark, 4 for 45; Cooper 2 for 15, 1 TD; Wilson, 1 for 22; Young, 1 for 14; Patton, 1 for 6; Ring, 1 for 3. *Cincinnati* – Ross, 11 for 104, 2 TD; Collinsworth, 5 for 107; Curtis, 3 for 42; Kreider, 2 for 36; Johnson, 2 for 8; Alexander, 2 for 3.
Punting: *San Francisco* – Miller, 4 for 46.3 average. *Cincinnati* – McInally, 3 for 43.7.
Punt Returns: *San Francisco* – Hicks, 1 for 6. *Cincinnati* – Fuller, 4 for 35.
Kickoff Returns: *San Francisco* – Hicks, 1 for 23; Lawrence, 1 for 17; Clark, 1 for 0. *Cincinnati* – Verser, 5 for 52; A Griffin, 1 for 0; Frazier, 1 for 0.
Interceptions: *San Francisco* – Hicks, 1 for 27; Wright, 1 for 25. *Cincinnati* – None.

Super Bowl XVI. Bengal QB Ken Anderson came to SB XVI from a season in which he passed for 3754 and 29 TDs. In the game he would add 300 more yards and two more TDs.

14
65

The San Francisco 49ers were the surprise of the NFC in 1981. Coach Bill Walsh had glued together quite a unit with an assortment of draft picks, free agents and trades. Finishing 2-14 in 1979, they surged to 13-3 over the 1981 regular season. The backbone of the team was an unsung defense, but the star of the show was quarterback Joe Montana. Since his college days at Notre Dame, he had shown a knack for coming back.

The playoffs that year offered ample opportunity to showcase the abilities of both facets of the 49ers' game – the unsung defense and Montana's come-from-behind, late-game heroics. In the end, both got their just rewards: Super Bowl rings.

Montana's big moment came against the Dallas Cowboys in the NFC championship game played at Candlestick Park on January 10, 1982, although trivia buffs will recall he threw three interceptions that day. The two teams jumped back and forth until Dallas took a 17-14 lead just before the half on a Tony Dorsett sweep. Things remained that way until the middle of the third quarter, when Cowboy quarterback Danny White threw an interception, which the 49ers used to set up the go-ahead touchdown, 21-17. Early in the fourth, Dallas tightened things up to 21-20 with a Rafael Septien field goal. Then rookie running back Walt Easley fumbled for the 49ers, the Cowboys took over at midfield and four plays later White threw tight end Doug Cosbie a 21-yard touchdown pass for a 27-21 lead.

Montana was known as a confidence man, but he promptly deflated the 49ers' tires by throwing an interception on the next possession. It was time for the San Francisco defense, which stopped the Cowboys' eat-the-clock plans and forced them to punt. Show Montana got the ball back at the 49er 11-yard line with 4:54 left. Montana and Walsh wisely used the ground game to eat up the Cowboys' prevent defense. If they showed signs of tightening, Montana drilled a quick one to his primary receivers – Freddie Solomon and Dwight Clark.

The moment of truth came at the Dallas six on third and three with 58 seconds left. Montana was to look for Solomon in the left of the end zone, but the primary receiver was covered, and the Dallas rush, led by 6-foot-9 Ed 'Too Tall' Jones, was bearing down. So Montana exited to his right, bought just enough time, and lofted a high one just as the Dallas boys crashed in. Dwight Clark, 6-foot-4, waiting at the back of the end zone, leaped up and grabbed the ball. Ray Wersching's conversion kick put the 49ers in the Super Bowl, 28-27.

The unlikeliest of Super Bowl opponents – San Francisco and the Cincinnati Bengals – had the unlikeliest setting: the Pontiac Superdome. The Bengals' transformation from a last-place team in 1980 to a first-place club in 1981 began with the introduction of their new tiger-striped helmets. Its strength, of course, was a new-found power in the offense. Veteran quarterback Ken Anderson had been a developing stalwart, and for 1981 he had saved his finest performance, completing 300 of 479 passes for 3754 yards and 29 touchdowns against only 10 interceptions. A real difference in the Cincinnati offense was rookie receiver Chris Collinsworth, who had a stunning 1009 yards receiving and 15 touchdowns. The power in the ground game came from bruiser fullback, Pete Johnson, a local favorite out of Ohio State who rushed for 1077 yards. Anderson was the team's second leading rusher with 320 yards on the season. The Bengals' 12-4 record included a 21-3 loss to San Francisco during the season, but Cincinnati had persisted in the playoffs, mainly on the strength of Anderson's consistency. He completed 14 of 21 passes for 192 yards and no interceptions in the first round meeting with the Buffalo Bills, and clinched a 28-21 victory in the fourth quarter with a 16-yard scoring pass to Collinsworth.

The AFC championship game was played in the sub-zero weather of Cincinnati's Riverfront Stadium, and that was enough to frost the passing game of San Diego's Dan Fouts and 'Air Coryell,' 27-7. Suddenly,

two previously undistinguished teams were meeting for the North's first Super Bowls. The media immediately seized on the fact that 49er coach Bill Walsh had been the architect of Cincinnati's passing game as an assistant to Paul Brown in the seventies. Anderson, in fact, credited Walsh with much of his development as a quarterback. When writing about Walsh, sportswriters all seemed to inject the description 'genius' into their copy. Montana expressed similar sentiments.

'Coach Walsh continually amazes me,' Montana said. 'From what I understand from talking to players on other teams, most teams have the same 20 or 25 plays, but we've always got new plays as well as dozens of old plays. Lots of games we'll be prepared to use 60 different plays. One game I remember we had over 100 plays. And then there's all our different formations, too.'

Finally given his chance as a head coach after

Left: *San Francisco kicker Ray Wersching made four FGs.*

Inset: *49er coach Bill Walsh.*

Top: *Go Bengals, go!*

Above: *49er QB Joe Montana, later named MVP , completed 14 of 22 passes for 157 yards and a TD, leading his team to its first SB victory. Montana was known for working well under stress.*

Left: *49er back Earl Cooper makes San Francisco's second TD on a Montana pass.*

Right: *TE Dan Ross scores the second Cincinnati TD.*

Below: *The AFC championship game that brought the Bengals to the Super Bowl was played in sub-zero weather. Behind the cloud of condensed breath: Charger Dan Fouts, losing QB.*

years in the league as an assistant, Walsh had made good on it. A big part of that success had been the development of Montana. The playoff game against Dallas had been a showcase for the quarterback. 'I did not mind being in that situation,' Montana said of his comeback against the Cowboys. 'I thought, "If we don't get it back, we don't win." But I never thought about it being a championship game.'

His coolness calmed those around him, said San Francisco offensive guard Randy Cross. 'He's not so far into the game that he loses perspective. He's rather detached. It's like he's able to do it in the third person.'

Walsh had drafted Montana and developed him despite the serious questions pro scouts had about Montana's strength as a passer. 'I can't find any negatives about Joe Montana's arm,' Walsh said in the days before the Super Bowl. 'Maybe the so-called experts can. People who say it's only an average arm are mistaken. And they always will be. Because his delivery is not a flick of the wrist like Terry Bradshaw's, they think it's not strong. He throws on the run while avoiding a pass rush, and he does not have to be totally set. He is not a moving platform like some others who are mechanical and can only do well when everything is just right. Joe performs just as well under stress.'

Beyond his 'genius,' a description Walsh came to resent, the San Francisco coach exhibited a common sense about the Super Bowl atmosphere: 'I don't think it's that traumatic for players to come to the Super Bowl. I don't buy the spectacle part. It's not a Cecil B DeMille thing. It's a football game for players. You have to go into a game like this with your best foot forward. You do the things that got you here, the things you do best. I think both teams will be conservative.' And he actually welcomed the location of Super Bowl XVI in Michigan, commenting that it was a better atmosphere for the big game.

Whereas Walsh was talkative, his Cincinnati counterpart, Forrest Gregg, was tight-lipped. The former all-pro lineman for Vince Lombardi made no bones about it. 'I think the players do a better job on me, keeping me loose,' he said at the team's hotel. 'I'm intense.'

At first, Super Bowl XVI was anything but that. San Francisco dominated early. Montana ran for a touchdown in the first quarter, passed for another in the second, and directed his team to two Ray Wersching field goals for a 20-0 halftime lead. But the offense wasn't the real story. The game was simply won in the first three quarters on key defensive plays, particularly a goal-line stand in the third when Anderson was leading his team back from the 20-0 deficit. After scoring a touchdown to narrow the lead to 20-7 in the third quarter, Anderson completed a big pass on his next possession to Cris Collinsworth at the 49er 14. The Bengals then changed weapons to big fullback Pete Johnson and battered to a first down at the three. Johnson then picked up two yards to the one, where the Bengals tried him again, this time over left guard. San Francisco lineman John Harty stopped him for no gain. Anderson then tried a pass, but was unable to find any open receiver in the end zone and had to settle for running back Charles Alexander at

Above: *Joe Montana dives over a tangle of bodies to score a 49er TD from the one.*

Right: *The game was played in an unlikely spot, Michigan's Pontiac Silverdome.*

Opposite left: *49er RB Ricky Patton led in rushing, with 55.*

Opposite right: *Cincinnati TE Dan Ross received 11 passes for a gain of 104 yards.*

the one. Linebacker Dan Bunz hit him high and wrestled him down for no gain. The Bengals went again to Johnson on fourth down, but the 49er defensive line wasn't in the mood to give ground.

'I really didn't think we could stop them,' said Jack Reynolds, the 49ers' inside linebacker. 'But what I thought and what we did were two different things. We stopped them by being real aggressive.' John Harry described the big play: 'They had momentum. The crowd was on their side. I was in the gap between Dave Lapham, their left guard, and Anthony Munoz, the left tackle. I knew I had to get under my man and get to Johnson. I threw my body in front of Johnson, twisted, grabbed his leg and pulled.'

'Johnson was coming at me,' said Lawrence Pillers, the defensive tackle for the 49ers. 'Mike Wilson was trying to block me out. I came down in the gap and under Wilson, and I saw a foot coming at me. I figured it was Johnson. It was. I grabbed the foot and hung on. I knew Jack Reynolds was behind me.'

From the momentum of a tremendous goal line stand, San Francisco went on to win its first Super Bowl, 26-21.

'We won,' Ronnie Lott said, 'because we got out on people. We made the plays. We made history today. We are part of history.'

'How good are we?' Reynolds asked. 'We're the world champions, aren't we?' For the game, Montana had completed 14 of 22 pass attempts for 157 yards and a touchdown. He was named the game's Most Valuable Player, prompting Walsh to tell reporters, 'Montana will be the great quarterback of the future. He is one of the coolest competitors of all time and he has just started. . . . I told the team at halftime that we would have to score at least 10 more points. If we had a 24-0 lead, it might've been enough, but a 20-0 lead was not enough, not against a great team like the Bengals.'

Dan Ross, the Bengals' tight end, commented on the awe-inspiring atmosphere. 'This was crazy,' he said. 'When I came out of the tunnel and on to the field of the Silverdome, I couldn't breathe. It was like I was star-struck. It wasn't all the lights of the Silverdome, or even the fans, but all of this and the knowledge that there are 100 million people sitting in their living rooms about to watch this. Suddenly, it hits you – the whole magnitude of it. . . . I was tight. I wasn't fluid like you are when you're on top of things. I missed a couple of blocks that made a difference. I dropped a pass, and another time I dropped a pass over the middle I normally tuck in.'

In the San Francisco locker room, the players, the executives, the coaches were celebrating the team's first-ever Super Bowl championship.

Amid the din, the phone was ringing. Walsh was nearest to the phone, so he picked it up. 'This is Ronald Reagan,' the caller said.

'Well, I thought it might be,' replied Walsh.

Super Bowl XVII

Washington Redskins 27, Miami Dolphins 17

30 January 1983
Rose Bowl, Pasadena, Calif.
Attendance: 103,667

Miami	7	10	0	0	—	17
Washington	0	10	3	14	—	27

Miami – Cefalo, 76, pass from Woodley (von Schamann kick).
Washington – Field goal, 31, Moseley.
Miami – Field goal, 20, von Schamann.
Washington – Garrett, 4, pass from Theismann (Moseley kick).
Miami – Walker, 98, kickoff return (von Schamann kick).
Washington – Field goal, 20, Moseley.
Washington – Riggins, 43, run (Moseley kick).
Washington – Brown, 6, pass from Theismann (Moseley kick).

Rushing: *Miami* – Franklin, 16 for 49; Woodley, 4 for 16; Nathan, 7 for 26; Harris, 1 for 1; Vigorito, 1 for 4. *Washington* – Riggins, 38 for 166, 1 TD; Harmon, 9 for 40; Walker, 1 for 6; Theismann, 3 for 20; Garrett, 1 for 44.
Passing: *Miami* – Woodley, 4 of 14 for 97, 1 TD, 1 int; Strock, 0 of 3 for 0. *Washington* – Theismann, 15 of 23 for 143, 2 TD, 2 int.
Receiving: *Miami* – Cefalo, 2 for 82, 1 TD; Harris, 2 for 15. *Washington* – Brown, 6 for 60, 1 TD; Warren, 5 for 28; Walker, 1 for 27; Riggins, 1 for 15; Garrett, 2 for 13, 1 TD.
Punting: *Miami* – Orosz, 6 for 37.8 average. *Washington* – Hayes, 4 for 42.
Punt Returns: *Miami* – Vigorito, 2 for 22. *Washington* – Nelms, 6 for 52.
Kickoff Returns: *Miami* – L Blackwood, 2 for 32; Walker, 4 for 190. *Washington* – Nelms, 2 for 44; Wonsley, 1 for 13.
Interceptions: *Miami* – Duhe, 1 for 0; L Blackwood, 1 for 0. *Washington* – Murphy, 1 for 0.

Super Bowl XVII saw Washington defeat Miami and win its first NFL championship since 1942.

VON SCHAMANN
5
FOSTER
79
88
57
68

In the early years of pro football the stars were often immortalized by their nicknames. Red 'Galloping Ghost' Grange. Bronko Nagurski. Elroy 'Crazy Legs' Hirsch. Byron 'Whizzer' White. Sam 'Slingin' Sammy' Baugh. Johnny 'Blood' McNally. That, of course, was in the days before television, when athletes seemed larger than life. Few such nicknames had survived in the glare of modern media. Broadway Joe Namath, perhaps. But not many more. Instead, the emphasis had shifted to group nicknames by the 1980s, as pro football dug into its heritage of hype. The result was a collision of monikers in Super Bowl XVII: the Killer Bees versus the Hawgs and Smurfs.

The Killer Bees were the Miami Dolphins' stinging defense, named because many of the starters – Lyle and Glenn Blackwood, Doug Betters, Bob Baumhower, Kim Bokamper, Bob Brudzinski – had last names starting with B. The Hawgs were the Washington Redskin offensive linemen, dubbed such because they averaged 270 pounds and grunted opponents out of the way. The Smurfs were the Redskins' diminutive receivers, Alvin Garrett and Charlie Brown.

The 1982 regular season, shortened to nine games by a players' strike, had brought a rematch of the 1973 Super Bowl. After a decade, Don Shula was still the Dolphins' coach. But the Redskins had a new leader, Joe Gibbs, a purveyor of the passing game who came to rely on the run for the 30 January Super Bowl in Pasaedena. If this sounds surprising, there was in fact a simple explanation for it.

Far left: *One of the surprises of the game was the power of the unheralded Redskin defense.*

Left: *In the second quarter WR Alvin Garrett races toward Washington's first TD.*

Below: *Who was that masked man? Fans called the Washington offensive line 'The Hawgs.' The Hawgs averaged 270 pounds.*

Right: *According to Skins fans little WRs Garrett (89) and Charlie Brown (87) were 'The Smurfs.' With them is 265-lb 'Hawg' tackle Garry Puetz (71).*

The reason for Gibbs' favoring the run was 33-year-old John Riggins, Washington's blend of power and speed at fullback on the field and craziness off it. Earlier in his career, as a New York Jet, he had sported a Mohawk haircut; other times he had worn his curly hair Afro style. Whatever the fad, he employed it for an impact. Riggins, a former University of Kansas star, had sat out the 1980 season over a contract dispute. His comeback in 1981 had been a slow one. But he had been a major factor in the Skins' 8-1 regular season record in 1982. By the playoffs that year he was in top form and in three playoff wins Riggins carried the ball 98 times for 444 yards, an average of more than 30 carries and 114 yards per game.

In interviews before the Super Bowl, reporters asked Riggins repeatedly what he thought of the Hawgs. 'I think they're a bunch of slobs,' he said, 'but they're my kind of guys.' Sportswriters were even more intrigued by his reputation for madcap antics. 'I wouldn't call them crazy,' he said. 'I'm just expressing myself. I like to do what I like to do at the moment. I'm spontaneous, but I like to think I'm always in control of the situation. . . . '

'He's a team guy,' said Gibbs, 'and very intelligent, very motivated. But he's going to set his own path in life. I think he prides himself in doing things a little different.' A big factor in Riggins' improved performance for the Redskins was Gibbs' decision to let him run the ball more. 'The more he got the ball,' said Gibbs, 'the better he was.'

'I'd like to carry a lot,' said Riggins, 'because it takes time to get my rhythm.' He would get plenty of chances to carry in the upcoming Super Bowl – 38, in fact – and no one would criticize his rhythm.

Another big part of the Redskins' emergence was their improved pass rush, featuring Dexter Manley, a fifth-round draft choice out of Oklahoma State who was a great surprise, despite his lack of modesty. 'I'm going to have a good game,' Manley said, 'because I owe it to myself. This is it. This is the last game. I don't want to come off the field and say I wish I had played better. If you want to be the best, you have to play the best.'

The Dolphins had come back to the Super Bowl after a nine-year absence. As with their last trip, they came with a so-so offense and a killer defense. Having much to do with that was the return of defensive coordinator Bill Arnsparger, who had come back to the Dolphins after an unsuccessful stint as head coach of the New York Giants.

'Basically, we're a three-man line team,' Don Shula said. 'We have our stunts. For example, Baumhower does not always go straight into the center. He'll go one way or the other, our defensive ends will step in or out, and our linebackers will compensate with their "games." Those are all parts of the sophistication of the three-man line.

The other strength in the Dolphins' defense was cornerbacks Don McNeal and Gerald Small. Their job was to control the Smurfs. 'Gerald and I talked last night about what problems they may give us because they're so small,' McNeal said of the Redskins. 'With their quickness, we may have to wait until they make

Left: *Redskin RB John Riggins (44) was the game's MVP. He rushed for 166, received for 15 more and scored one TD.*

Right: *Don Shula and some of the members of Miami's 'Killer Bees' defense at the opening ceremonies.*

Below: *Miami QB David Woodley.*

their moves before we jam them. I've never played guys that small. After the jam, I don't know. We'll have to feel our way through the game.'

Arnsparger was just as worried about holding down the motion in the Redskin offense. 'They move around a lot,' he said. 'They probably have more movement in their offense than any team we faced. You have to watch Theismann roll out. Then, for Riggins, they have different types of blocking. They bring the tight end in. They have Walker, a tight end, he goes side to side, and while this is going on the ball's snapped. It's an attention-getter.'

More than anything, the Super Bowl appearance accentuated Miami's lost promise. After winning two straight Super Bowls in 1972 and 1973, Don Shula watched his great Dolphins team fall apart, with players jumping to the World Football League. The comedown had changed Shula's approach to the game but hadn't dampened his competitive fires.

'Don has changed a little,' veteran offensive guard Bob Kuechenberg offered for reporters. 'Our society has changed. I think of Vince Lombardi, one of the greatest all-time coaches, very rigid, very demanding. There are times when I would go through a brick wall, but Don Shula has transcended that era of asking a player to go through a brick wall without asking questions. Coach Shula is more relaxed now. He's enjoying the hunt. He still wants to win but he's able to smile and crack a joke.' To communicate the importance of the big game, Kuechenberg told his younger teammates: 'The Super Bowl is singularly what makes pro football worthwhile. You guys in the press laugh when I say you don't play for the money. Look how short the average career is – four-point-two years. You couldn't sacrifice to play unless you loved it. This week and this game make it all worthwhile.'

Yet the meaning in this Super Bowl would belong to Riggins and the Redskins. The big back would surpass all expectations, teaming with the Hawgs to become the battering ram that broke down Miami's defense.

The Dolphins scored first on a 76-yard bomb from quarterback David Woodley to Jimmy Cefalo. Washington answered with a Mark Moseley field

goal. Miami then drove to a first down just inside the Washington 10, but the Redskin defense turned nasty. On fourth down, Uwe von Schamann kicked a field goal for a 10-3 lead. Theismann laced together a series of deceptive plays on an 80-yard drive, completed by a four-yard scoring pass to Garrett with just over two minutes left in the first half.

With the score tied at 10, Miami's receiving team struck back, freeing Fulton Walker for a 98-yard touchdown. It was the only time that a kickoff had been returned for a touchdown in a Super Bowl. Washington rushed back at the end of the half but ran out of time on the Miami 16 trailing 17-10.

In the third quarter, Moseley kicked another field goal, bringing the Redskins to 17-13. The Washington defense continued to dominate, holding the Dolphins' offense to almost nothing. It was the Miami defense that nearly put the game away with two minutes remaining in the period. Theismann was attempting a pass from his own 18 when Bokamper rushed in and tipped the ball. The big nosetackle was poised to catch the tip and run in for a score when Theismann alertly jumped in and knocked the ball away.

The fourth quarter would belong to Riggins and the Redskins. They were driving into Dolphin territory and faced a fourth and one at the Miami 43. Washington ran Riggins left and used a man in motion to draw cornerback Don McNeal away from the coverage area. Miami was in a six-man line, and when McNeal realized the vulnerability he attempted to regain his position. But he slipped and was unable to get more than a hand on Riggins, which of course wasn't enough to stop Big John. 'Riggo's Run,' as the play became known, went for 43 yards and the go-ahead touchdown.

'John has been running good throughout the playoffs, after being kind of up and down during the regular season,' said Russ Grimm, the Redskins' left guard. 'He's hard to bring down. He runs with a lot of authority. . . . They changed defenses on the play. When they lined up, they were in the '34,' which is their basic defense. Then they called timeout, and when they lined up again, they were in the '60,' in other words, with six linemen, with gaps. The play hits off tackle, and Riggins had one guy to beat, and he outran him down the sidelines.'

McNeal, the Dolphins' fine cornerback, missed the tackle. 'I wanted to make him bounce outside,' he said, 'but I never did get my arms all the way around him. He was like a train. I didn't get my head in front of him, and he just ran through me. I missed a tackle that got them ahead. It's just one of those things. Somebody had to be remembered. Why not me?'

Ten minutes were left, and the Redskins used them running Riggins right at the Dolphins. They ate up the clock and digested another touchdown for a 27-17 victory, Washington's first championship since 1942. Riggins had finished with a Super Bowl record 166 yards on 38 carries, which was MVP material and pretty near Hawg Heaven. 'I guess a guy fell down,' Riggins said of his run. 'Another guy couldn't quite hold on. That's it. I'm very happy. At least for tonight, Ron's the President, but I'm the king.'

'In the second half we just had to control the line and we did,' Dexter Manley told reporters after the game. 'We believed in ourselves and our Mack Truck, John Riggins.'

Top left: *Riggins is smothered.*

Top center: *Skins, including Joe Theismann (7), who made the pass, cheer Garrett's TD.*

Far left below: *The Skins win! In the foreground is guard Fred Dean; behind, defensive end Dexter Manley.*

Left: *Skins QB Joe Theismann gets set to pass over a leaping A J Duhe (77).*

Above: *Skins owner Jack Kent (l) and coach Joe Gibbs get a congratulatory call from the White House.*

Fortunately, the Mack truck moved out of Washington's motion offense. 'They had so much movement that sometimes we got confused," Miami's A J Duhe said. 'They also used a lot of long counts and had guys moving. They have a big, strong offensive line, and they were knocking us off the ball. I wasn't sure what they would do some of the time. They executed better. It wasn't a case of too much Riggins, but he's an awfully good runner.'

'You have to give a lot of credit to the Washington offense and John Riggins,' Shula said. 'He was a dominant force. And the Redskins' offensive line had a great surge in the second half.'

'The key to this game was our ability to run the ball,' said Theismann. 'If Riggins runs well, it opens up the passing game for us. We just turned our Hogs loose today. I'm very confident about this football team. . . . The guys up front did a great job for John. The special teams came through when they had to, and the defense shut them down all afternoon. This is a dream come true, the greatest day of my life. I love to play football. I felt I could have knocked the eyes out of a fly today if I had to. I just hope they'll buy us the biggest and the gaudiest Super Bowl rings. The memories and the ring, no one can take that away.'

'We totally dominated them,' said offensive lineman George Starke. 'I'm afraid I'm going to have to say we were the better team. We didn't trick them. We did nothing fancy. We knocked the defense out of there. We block, and Riggins runs.'

Super Bowl XVIII

Los Angeles Raiders 38, Washington Redskins 9

22 January 1984
Tampa Stadium
Attendance: 72,920

Washington	0	3	6	0	—	9
Los Angeles	7	14	14	3	—	38

Los Angeles – Jensen recovered blocked punt in end zone (Bahr kick).
Los Angeles – Branch, 12, pass from Plunkett (Bahr kick).
Washington – Field goal, 24, Moseley.
Los Angeles – Squirek, 5, interception return (Bahr kick).
Washington – Riggins, 1, run (kick blocked).
Los Angeles – Allen, 5, run (Bahr kick).
Los Angeles – Allen, 74, run (Bahr kick).
Los Angeles – Field goal, 21, Bahr.

Rushing: *Washington* – Riggins, 26 for 64, 1 TD; Theismann, 3 for 18; J Washington, 3 for 8. *Los Angeles* – Allen, 20 for 191, 2 TD; King, 3 for 12; Hawkins, 3 for 6; Pruitt, 5 for 17; Plunkett, 1 for –2; Willis, 1 for 7.
Passing: *Washington* – Theismann, 16 of 35 for 243, 2 int. *Los Angeles* – Plunkett, 16 of 25 for 172, 1 TD
Receiving: *Washington* – Didier, 5 for 65; J Washington, 3 for 20; Garrett, 1 for 17; Brown, 3 for 93; Giaquinto, 2 for 21; Monk, 1 for 26; Riggins, 1 for 1. *Los Angeles* – Allen, 2 for 18; King, 2 for 8; Christensen, 4 for 32; Branch, 6 for 94, 1 TD; Hawkins, 2 for 20.
Punting: *Washington* – Hayes, 7 for 37 average. *Los Angeles* – Guy, 7 for 42.7.
Punt Returns: *Washington* – Green, 1 for 34; Giaquinto, 1 for 1. *Los Angeles* – Watts, 1 for 0; Pruitt, 1 for 8.
Kickoff Returns: *Washington* – Garrett, 5 for 100; Grant, 1 for 32; Kimball, 1 for 0. *Los Angeles* – Pruitt, 1 for 17.
Interceptions: *Washington* – None. *Los Angeles* – Squirek, 1 for 5, 1 TD; Haynes, 1 for 0.

Joe Theismann, John Riggins and company returned to face the Raiders in Super Bowl XVIII. It would not prove a happy experience for them.

The football world can be forgiven for thinking the Washington Redskins were a cinch to repeat as Super Bowl champions. They had given pro football some of its more thrilling moments in running to a 14-2 record during the 1983 season. They scored 17 points in the final six minutes to overtake the Los Angeles Raiders, 37-35, October 2 in Washington's RFK Stadium.

Their Monday night games were even more exciting, if less productive. The Redskins lost two, 31-30, to Dallas, and 48-47 to the Green Bay Packers, a masterpiece of a game that featured a winning kick by Jan Stenerud.

All in all, however, it was a red-letter regular season for the Skins, as they racked up an NFL record of 541 points over 16 games, the most impressive offensive display ever. John Riggins rushed for 1347 yards and Joe Washington another 772. The air game soared on Joe Theismann's 3714 yards passing. He had completed 60 percent of his passes and rang up 29 touchdown tosses against 11 interceptions. Washington's rise to the top of the league had been a streak of beauty and precision, which left them and their fans all the more unprepared for their humiliating fall.

The Redskins didn't so much break records as they did the LA Rams' backs, 51-7, in the first round of the playoffs, which only served to increase the talk of invincibility. A narrow win over the 49ers, 24-21, in the NFC championship the following week quieted the talk some. Their performance was a typical playoff showing by the Redskins. Riggins rushed for 123 yards and two touchdowns, and Theismann threw for 229 yards and another touchdown as Washington took a 21-0 third quarter lead. Then at the opening of the fourth when San Francisco's Joe Montana zapped the weak Redskin secondary for three touchdown passes to tie the game at 21. Staggering, Theismann somehow directed the offense to the winning field goal by Mark Moseley with 40 seconds left.

Meanwhile, over in the AFC, the Los Angeles Raiders were shattering everybody else's playoff hopes after finishing the regular season 12-4. The old man of the AFL, Jim Plunkett, had thrown for nearly 3000 yards and Marcus Allen had rushed for 1014.

All that continued in the playoffs. Plunkett passed for a snappy 232 yards and Allen rushed for 121 yards and two touchdowns in knocking off the Steelers, 38-10.

Allen upped his numbers to 154 yards in the AFC title game against the Seattle Seahawks, and Plunkett threw for 214. But the Raider defense did the real number on Seattle, slamming down the ground game and ripping off quarterbacks Dave Kreig and Jim Zorn for five interceptions. Finally it ended, 31-14.

The Super Bowl matchup brought the pre-game speculation to new levels. First, the regular season game had been a thriller. And while the Redskins

had dominated the schedule, the Raiders had devastated good teams in the playoffs.

'Both of these teams have very talented big-play people,' Redskins coach Joe Gibbs told reporters. 'Yet the problem is, they're matched up against excellent defenses. That's why the game could come down to inches – a guy makes a big catch on his fingertips or the ball gets batted away.'

Raiders coach Tom Flores wanted nothing more than another shot at Washington. 'We have prepared for everything,' he said. 'We know what they have done in recent games, and we even practiced against some things they haven't done. We have to be ready for anything.' The rise of the Redskins and their hopes to become the team of the eighties became the focus of news stories in the week. Of particular interest was the role of their 71-year-old owner, Jack Kent Cooke, the former owner of the Los Angeles Lakers. 'Mr Cooke has given us everything we need to win,' said Bobby Beathard, the Redskins' general manager. 'He enabled us to get Joe Gibbs, the coach I wanted to replace Jack Pardee in 1981 after I expressed my feelings that we had to make a change.'

Long known in the league for his ability, Gibbs found the immediate climate for winning in Washington. 'Mr Cooke is the boss, he's in charge of the money,' Gibbs said. 'But very few coaches can keep any player regardless of the money that player is making or what round he was drafted in. We've cut

Left: *Raider QB Jim Plunkett hands off to RB Marcus Allen, who made two TDs in the game.*

Above: *Coach Tom Flores of the roughneck Raiders.*

Below: *Skins QB Joe Theismann confers with coach Joe Gibbs. Theismann passed for 243, yet Washington lost by the biggest margin in Super Bowl history until SB XXII.*

Right: *Theismann fades back as Skins RB Joe Washington dashes forward. Just before the half an intercepted pass meant for Washington gave the Raiders their third TD.*

Above: *Raider publicity men promoted the team's black and silver colors into a 'Darth Vaders of Football' image that many people felt was a little too theatrical, if not corny.*

guys drafted in the second or third rounds and kept free agents. I've also kept guys making $150,000 who aren't that much better than guys making $60,000 that we cut.'

One of the big questions upon Gibbs' arrival was the status of quarterback Joe Theismann. Quarterback and coach met quickly. 'I didn't expect answers,' Theismann said. 'I didn't expect questions. I had hoped to just sit down and find something. I know we're all bears when we wake up, but he was nice. We sat down and just started to talk and the conversation just flowed.'

'I was looking for a quarterback that I could more or less base my future on,' Gibbs recalled. 'And I think Joe was looking for a coach that he could base his future on. Both of us were trying to see if we were the same guy. I was trying to figure out how good a quarterback he was and how important football was to him.'

It didn't take Beathard long to know he had made the right decision in Gibbs. After some initial adjustments, Gibbs found a way to win. And on the wings of that success, the personality of the Redskins emerged. It was a mixed bag of Hawgs, Smurfs and characters, particularly John Riggins. If anything, the Redskins seemed too wholesome for a football team, almost too squeaky clean. Observers wondered how that might work against them in a championship matchup with the roughneck Raiders.

Asked about this, Riggins said: 'Maybe they like their reputation. But they go to church and have wives and things like that. They're not as big and ugly as they would have people believe.'

If the Raiders did have a nice guy, he was their coach. 'We may have a reputation as an intimidating football team, but we're no cheap-shot players,' Flores said. 'We had our share of penalties, but we're not dirty football players.'

Left: *In the first quarter TE Derrick Jensen blocked a punt by Skin Jeff Hayes and recovered it in the end zone for the first Raider score.*

Right: *WR Cliff Branch gave the Raiders their second score with a 12-yard TD on a pass from Jim Plunkett.*

Once considered in danger of losing his job, Flores, a former Raider quarterback, had become the stabilizing factor on a team whose members were often considered football misfits. 'After we won the Super Bowl three years ago,' Flores said, 'people around Oakland waved to me or honked their horns. All that attention was the greatest feeling I had ever experienced. . . . We've got an old-fashioned offense. We still use two backs, we don't use much motion, we still like to throw to our wide receivers. We attack – on offense, on defense, on special teams.'

It sounded homey and old-fashioned, but few people bought it. The Raiders, instead, were portrayed as an extension of Al Davis, who was embroiled in a lawsuit with Commissioner Pete Rozelle and the league over the decision to move the team to Los Angeles from Oakland. Many people figured Davis called all the shots, right down to the game plan. 'Al Davis is a football man,' Flores said. 'Al wants to know everything that's going on – the draft, the personnel. He's not involved in putting together the game plan, but he'll offer suggestions. He's there daily, at practice, at training camp. And then he goes home and worries.'

Despite his intensity and involvement, no one – players or coaches – seemed to resent Davis' presence. 'Coach Davis is a genius,' said Lester Hayes, the all-pro cornerback. 'His realm of knowledge is astounding. He knows the cornerback's technique, he knows the nose-guard's technique. . . . He does a lot of whispering to the players and his whispering is very helpful to us.'

To say the least, the Raiders lived up to their promise in Super Bowl XVIII. The outcome left the Redskins stunned and elicited comparisons to their 73-0 loss to the Bears in 1940. It wasn't quite that bad. But it was bad. Raiders classy back Marcus Allen rushed for a Super Bowl record 191 yards, and the LA

defense, led by Howie Long, Lyle Alzado, and others, wrapped up the Washington offense for a 38-9 win. With just five minutes gone in the first quarter, the Raiders' Derrick Jensen blocked a punt by Washington's Jeff Hayes and covered the loose ball in the end zone for a 7-0 LA lead. Plunkett opened the second quarter with a touchdown pass for a 14-0 lead, and Washington's answer was a Mark Moseley field goal. With 12 seconds left in the half, Raiders linebacker Jack Squirek intercepted a Theismann sideline pass to Joe Washington and stepped five yards into the end zone for a 21-3 lead. Riggins scored in the third quarter, but Marcus Allen answered for the Raiders with a pair of touchdowns, including a 74-yard beauty that snuffed out the beast in the Redskins.

The famed Washington ground game had managed only 90 yards against the Raider defense. 'We're the Slaughterhouse Seven,' Long said of the Raiders' front defense. 'We never had a hawg that tasted so good.'

'They are a great football team,' Rozelle told Davis afterwards. 'And they sure showed it today.' Flores agreed: 'We just played a great football game. We dominated them. There's nothing better than feeling you can do what you want and dgoing it.'

'They put their linebackers right next to the line of scrimmage. We couldn't get any momentum going,' Riggins told reporters. 'I'm not sure I had 20-20 vision. I made more than one bad 'read.' I feel there was daylight there. I just didn't see it. It just seemed nothing went right today. We got stopped. They had seven people up tight at the line. You've got to have more power to surge up, and they've got big linebackers. Their corners weren't even supporting the run. They were just playing our receivers one-on-one.'

Al Davis was a picture of joy afterward with the Lombardi trophy. 'I love the Raiders,' he said. 'It's my life.' Asked if he thought it was ironic that his team had won the title while he was battling the league in court, Davis bristled, 'I don't think it's irony. What's the irony? I don't want to detract from this game. I don't think anyone enjoys court battles. We should be allowed to do what's right. We'll go into that in a little while, in two weeks.'

The Redskins were left searching for a reason for their demise. 'The wind was a factor, especially early in the game,' Theismann said. 'But even more of a factor was the Raiders' defense. Their cornerbacks, Mike Haynes and Lester Hayes, played tough. They shut our wide passing game down. By them pressing our receivers so much, you had to throw the ball extremely accurately. We weren't getting much yardage on first down. Everybody talks about third-down plays, but first-down plays are equally important. With second and 7 or second and 8, the Raiders were forcing us into passing situations. And the way their cornerbacks were covering our receivers, it made everything tougher. That interception at the end of the first half hurt us, no doubt about that, but it

Opposite left: *Mark Moseley gave the Redskins their first score with a 24-yard FG.*

Opposite right: *Linebacker Rod Martin. The Oakland defense completely undid the 'Hawgs'.*

Above: *Plunkett takes aim. He threw for 172 and a TD.*

Left: *The second of Raider Marcus Allen's TDs was made at the end of a 72-yard run.*

didn't discourage us. We came in here at halftime and never mentioned it. If anything, I think it made us more determined. When the second half started, we went out and drove right down the field for a touchdown. But then the Raiders came right back and scored. That's what hurt us more than the interception – that as soon as we scored in the second half, the Raiders scored too.'

Allen had perhaps the finest day of all, complete with the MVP Award, the Super Bowl rushing record and an $18,000 winner's check. 'I set very high standards for myself,' he said, 'higher than anyone else, and I was impatient because I wasn't reaching them. Then at about the eleventh or twelfth game of the season I just told myself to relax, and that's when I started coming on.'

It was a great victory. The Raiders had won by the biggest margin in Super Bowl history.

Super Bowl XIX

San Francisco 49ers 38, Miami Dolphins 16

20 January 1985
Stanford Stadium, Palo Alto, Calif.
Attendance: 84,059

Miami	10	6	0	0	—	16
San Francisco	7	21	10	0	—	38

Miami – Field goal, 37, von Schamann.
San Francisco – Monroe, 33, pass from Montana (Wersching kick).
Miami – D Johnson, 2, pass from Marino (von Schamann kick).
San Francisco – Craig, 8, pass from Montana (Wersching kick).
San Francisco – Montana, 6, run (Wersching kick).
San Francisco – Craig, 2, run (Wersching kick).
Miami – Field goal, 31, von Schamann.
Miami – Field goal, 30, von Schamann.
San Francisco – Field goal, 27, Wersching.
San Francisco – Craig, 16, pass from Montana (Wersching kick).

Rushing: *Miami* – Bennett, 3 for 7; Nathan, 5 for 18; Marino, 1 for 0. *San Francisco* – Tyler, 13 for 65; Craig, 15 for 58; 1 TD; Montana, 5 for 59, 1 TD; Harn, 5 for 20; Cooper, 1 for 4; Solomon, 1 for 5.
Passing: *Miami* – Marino, 29 of 50 for 318, 1 TD, 2 int. *San Francisco* – Montana, 24 of 35 for 331, 3 TD.
Receiving: *Miami* – Nathan, 10 for 83; D Johnson, 3 for 28, 1 TD; Clayton, 6 for 92; Duper, 1 for 11; Rose, 6 for 73; Moore, 2 for 17; Cefalo, 1 for 14. *San Francisco* – Tyler, 4 for 70; D Clark, 6 for 77; Craig, 7 for 77, 2 TD; Monroe, 1 for 33, 1 TD; Francis, 5 for 60; Solomon, 1 for 14.
Punting: *Miami* – Roby, 6 for 39.3 average. *San Francisco* – Runager, 3 for 32.7.
Punt Returns: *Miami* – Walker, 2 for 15. *San Francisco* – McLemore, 5 for 51.
Kickoff Returns: *Miami* – Hardy, 2 for 31; Walker, 4 for 93; Hill, 1 for 16. *San Francisco* – Harmon, 2 for 24; Monroe, 1 for 16; McIntyre, 1 for 0.
Interceptions: *Miami* – None. *San Francisco* – Wright, 1 for 0; Williamson, 1 for 0.

Going into Super Bowl XIX Dan Marino and the Miami offense looked unstoppable, but the 49ers didn't see it that way.

MARINO
13
57
NEWMAN
64

It was a bad year for records. They fell like tackling dummies over the course of the 1984 season, a trend that carried right through Super Bowl XIX at Stanford Stadium. Just about every kind of record – passing, rushing, receiving – was vulnerable, and most of the big ones fell: The Chicago Bears' Walter Payton bypassed Jim Brown's record for career rushing yardage of 12,312 yards; Miami quarterback Dan Marino threw for 48 touchdown passes, blowing right by YA Tittle's single season total of 36, and passed for 5084 yards, becoming the first player to go beyond 5000 yards; Mark Clayton, Marino's prime target, caught a record 18 touchdown passes; Rams running back Eric Dickerson beat O J Simpson's single-season rushing record of 2003 yards by piling up 2105; Washington's Art Monk caught 106 passes, breaking Charley Hennigan's record 101 catches; Charlie Joiner of San Diego claimed the lead in career receptions, finishing with 657, well ahead of Charley Taylor's 649 catches; and the Bears' defense set a record with 72 quarterback sacks. The San Francisco 49ers set a record of regular season wins by going 15-1, a harvest of victories that led to three members of the 49er offensive line – Randy Cross, Keith Fahnhorst and Fred Quillan – being named all-pro. Their efforts helped running back Wendell Tyler rush for more than 1200 yards over 16 games. Behind that and Joe Montana's passing (he completed 279 of 432 attempts for a 65 percent completion rate, grossing 3630 yards, 28 touchdown passes and 10 interceptions), San Francisco rang up a conference-leading 475 points. On defense, the 49ers entire secondary – Ronnie Lott, Eric Wright, Carlton Williamson and Dwight Hicks – picked up Pro Bowl invitations. Only a three-point loss to the Pittsburgh Steelers on October 15 marred their record.

Yet for the most part, that performance went largely unnoticed because Miami's Dan Marino, in only his second year as a pro, was the rage of the season's news coverage. With their Killer B defense bolstering their offensive outburst, the Dolphins riddled their first 11 opponents before losing to San Diego in overtime. They stalled briefly with another loss, to the Los Angeles Raiders, and finished the season 14-2. Their offense had gunned up 513 points, highest in the NFL.

To say the least, Marino, a late first-round pick out of the University of Pittsburgh, had taken the NFL by storm. At the close of the 1984 regular season, he was viewed as something of a miracle worker. 'The things he does even amaze his receivers,' Miami's Jimmy Cefalo said. 'If you're open, you think you have to wait for the ball but you never do. He just gets you the ball so quick. You look up, and the ball is there every time.'

Beyond his arm, his teammates cited Marino's leadership in the huddle. Marino threw two interceptions in the Dolphins' first-round playoff game with Seattle, but he tempered that with three touchdown passes, as Miami advanced handily, 31-10.

In the AFC title game, he passed for 421 yards and four touchdowns as the Dolphins outlasted Pittsburgh, 45-28.

The 49ers' path to the Super Bowl was blocked by two of football's finest defenses, by two teams rapidly developing as prime contenders, the New York Giants and the Chicago Bears. Against the Giants, Montana struck for two first-quarter touchdown passes, then battled the New York secondary (they intercepted three of his passes) the rest of the way. San Francisco won, 21-10.

In the NFC championship game, the Bears' defense was brutal, but their offense, with quarterback Jim McMahon out with an injury, was ineffective. The

Right: *The game was held in California's Stanford Stadium.*

Opposite above: *Dolphin Dan Marino prepares to take the snap from Dwight Stephenson. Marino had had a spectacular season, breaking NFL records in touchdown passes (48) and passing yardage (5084).*

49ers wore them down, scoring in every quarter, for a 23-0 win.

Coach Bill Walsh had a shot at his second Super Bowl title in four years, which was enough to bring the resurrection of his depiction by the media as a genius. 'I don't know if he's a genius,' said Matt Cavanaugh, the 49ers' backup quarterback. 'But he's a damn good coach, that's what he is. He knows how to handle players. He gives everyone a chance to play. If you're an alternate and he has a play designed for you, that keeps you ready. That's pretty smart.'

Regardless, the football world continued to be impressed by his rapid transformation of the 49ers from pitiful to powerful. 'In 1982,' said Walsh, 'I thought from weariness that I couldn't go another year as coach and general manager. I talked to many people, including friends in coaching, and decided to smooth out the edges and stay. Now I have two jobs again, and it's still asking too much to do both of them. But we've gone from a not-very-good-team in 1978 and 1979 to a world-championship team in 1982. Now we've matured and we're a little more corporate, a little more balanced.'

The primary factor in that balance, of course, was quarterback Joe Montana, now 28, now an NFL veteran. 'Montana is such a great athlete,' Don Shula said. 'He's a pocket passer, he comes out by design on the rollout and the bootleg, and he makes plays on the scramble. He'll wiggle around and come up with the big play. Against Joe Montana, you have to be contain-conscious.'

'Joe's not a scintillating personality in the huddle, he's not a rah-rah screaming type,' San Francisco offensive lineman Randy Cross said. 'He doesn't get down on his blockers or on hos receivers, but if he gets sacked or a receiver drops a ball, he lets you know.'

There was, however, just a hint of disrespect of Montana from the Dolphins. Lyle Blackwood, the Miami free safety, suggested that Montana's tendencies could be read easily by defenders. 'I'm not going to tell you what they are,' Blackwood told reporters. 'But when some quarterbacks are going to pass, they will walk out of the huddle a different way than when they're going to call a running play. Sometimes they'll bend over the center a different way, sometimes they don't look around as much, but Montana does a good job of looking over the whole field.'

The Miami defense wasn't so concerned about Montana as it was about the rest of the 49er offense. 'I think we'll see them try to establish their running game,' said Miami nosetackle Bob Baumhower. 'I think they'll use that to set up their passing game, and they'll use a lot of play-action fakes to get a better running game and more effective passing. We have had problems with controlling the run, although we've done better lately.'

John Madden, the CBS commentator, accurately focused his thoughts on San Francisco's defense. 'The 49ers play a hard defense,' he said. 'They'll rush Marino hard, try to pressure him, and they'll go after his receivers.' That would be inevitable, Madden said, because San Francisco could not afford to allow Marino to operate. 'Never let him get comfortable,' Madden said. 'If you do, he'll kill you.'

Left: *49er coach Bill Walsh.*

Right: *In the regular season three members of the 49er's offensive line had been named all-pro: Fred Quillan (56), Randy Cross (51) and Keith Fahnhorst (71).*

Above left: *QB Joe Montana hands off to RB Wendell Tyler.*

Above right: *Uwe von Schamann kicked 10 of Miami's 16 points.*

Right: *49er RB Roger Craig scored a Super Bowl-record three TDs. Together, Craig and Tyler rushed for 123 yards and received for 147 more. In all, the 49ers rushed for 211 yards.*

For his part, Walsh was well aware of the challenge facing his defense. 'It's strictly Marino's passing that is the one element that is so brilliant, so dynamic, that you become obsessed with trying to deal with it,' Walsh explained to reporters. 'He's overwhelming.' To say the least, the 49er defense relished the opportunity to meet Marino. Unfortunately for the Dolphins, Joe Montana and the rest of the San Francisco team tired quickly of hearing how great Miami was in the pre-game hype.

Miami opened with their strength, as Marino's arm took them downfield in seven plays to set up a 37-yard field goal by Uwe von Schamann. Montana answered by rolling out and lacing a scoring pass to running back Carl Monroe for a 7-3 lead. Marino upped the pot with another drive, 70 yards in six plays, capped by a two-yard touchdown pass for a 10-7 lead at the end of the first quarter.

But San Francisco hammered Miami's hopes in the second with three straight touchdowns. Montana passed for one, ran for another and handed off to Roger Craig for the third. The Dolphins punched up two field goals before the half, but the damage had been done. They trailed, 28-16, and it would get no better.

The 49ers added a field goal and another Montana to Craig touchdown pass in the third, while their defense shut the Dolphins down and out the rest of the way. The 49ers had sealed the Dolphins' tomb, 38-16. A profoundly disappointed Marino had thrown for 318 yards but also had two crucial interceptions. His 50 passing attempts and 29 completions were both Super Bowl records, among a host of new marks set on the afternoon.

Montana, ever the Golden Boy, had set the biggest, completing 24 of 35 attempts for a Super Bowl record 331 yards and three touchdowns, enough for everybody's MVP Award. In addition, he had set a record for yards rushing by a quarterback, 59. Alas Miami had attempted only nine rushes, a Super Bowl low. The San Francisco ground game, balanced between backs Wendell Tyler and Roger Craig, contributed 211 yards to the cause. And Craig's three touchdowns was another Super Bowl record. The 49ers' 537 net yards was the most ever by a Super Bowl team.

'He is the best quarterback around today, no question,' receiver Dwight Clark rhapsodized about Montana for reporters afterward. 'The best in the game today,' Walsh joined in. 'He is number one in assertiveness, leadership, and he has those quick feet.' 'Montana was outstanding in every way, said Shula, who had appeared in his sixth Super Bowl game, also a record. 'Every time we tried to put some pressure on him, he scrambled for a big play on his own or he bought time to hit one of his receivers. He hurt us in every way. He broke the record and did the job. When you get beat the way we got beat, you have to take your hat off to them and that's what I'll do. Defensively, we never stopped them.'

Montana indicated that the pre-game buildup of Marino had affected the 49ers. 'The whole offensive

33
40

unit, all we heard about was Marino, how to stop them,' Montana said. 'Nobody said anything about our offense. Inside, we knew we had an offense, too. Nobody was thinking about how to stop us.'

But in reality it was every bit as much a defensive victory. The 49ers had shut down the most powerful passing game in the history of football. 'The key was playing their early runs with the nickel (five defensive backs),' George Seifret, the 49er defensive co-ordinator, told reporters. 'We got into it a little sooner than we might have anticipated when it became evident that it was going to be a passing game.'

Shula saw it the same way. 'Early in the game we didn't use a huddle and we scored a touchdown,' he said. 'That made the 49ers decide to go to a four-man line and six defensive backs. We got a lot of that at the end of the season and felt we would get it today. We didn't go to the hurry-up offense when they switched to a four-man front. We tried to get some runs against it but the runs we used didn't work. They also had the lead, and we were fighting that. Our offense has been slowed down this season. But it was stopped for the first time today. Offensively, it was our poorest game of the year. We didn't make things happen.'

After the buildup of the big year, Marino seemed unprepared for the letdown of defeat. 'I didn't make the plays or something,' he said. 'I had the chances, but I didn't make the throws. Their defense played me better than anybody all year. They got the job done. I probably could have played a better game. We knew what we had to do, but they took us right out of our game. We all had great games this season. Today takes away from it. We can't be champions. We just didn't have it today. They were able to get some pressure on us and cover our receivers well. The chance we did have, when guys were open, sometimes I didn't hit them. We didn't play as well as we were capable of playing. That's probably because they dictated some things to us as far as their four-man line and playing five and six and seven defensive backs. We knew going in they had an excellent secondary and they played very well today. They should be given a lot of credit because they're the world champs, and they did what they had to do to win.'

TV analyst and former Philadelphia Eagles coach Dick Vermeil summed it up adequately: 'Well, it doesn't take much of an expert to analyze what happened in this football game. After the first quarter, Miami was never really in the game. Dan Marino brought them to the Super Bowl. But there was no way any one guy could bring them through. He didn't get enough help. The 49ers' offensive and defensive

Left: *The 49er's Ray Wersching kicked one field goal and five extra points in the game.*

Above: *Coach Don Shula with his disappointed Dolphins.*

Top: *Roger Craig makes a one-handed catch. His game total receiving was seven for 77.*

lines won it. Montana had time to throw and, when he didn't, he ran well. In the first half, he had three crucial scrambling plays, and all led to touchdowns. If they had stopped him on those plays, they would've stopped the drives. What made the difference was when the 49ers made their adjustment on defense in the first period. It looked, at that point, as though the Dolphins had come into the game trying to prove that they were indeed the best passing team in football. And they showed plenty during their scoring drive. Marino went 5 for 5 passing, and they shot half the length of the field without even going into the huddle. That drive gave them the lead, 10-7. But it gave San Francisco the clue they needed: This was a passing game the Dolphins were playing. So, on the next series, the 49ers jumped out of their three-man front on defense and went into a four-man front. That's what you do against the pass. That's what you do on third and long when it's clearly a passing situation. And that's what the 49ers did. They played a third-down defense every time for the rest of the game.'

For Montana, there was much to relish. 'We told Joe to take it when he could see it.' Bill Walsh said later. 'Dan Marino's a great young quarterback, but my feeling is that Joe Montana is the greatest quarterback today, maybe the greatest of all time.'

Super Bowl XX

Chicago Bears 46, New England Patriots 10

26 January 1986
Louisiana Superdome, New Orleans
Attendance: 73,818

Chicago	13	10	21	2	—	46
New England	3	0	0	7	—	10

New England – Field goal, 36, Franklin.
Chicago – Field goal, 28, Butler.
Chicago – Field goal, 24, Butler.
Chicago – Suhey, 11, run (Butler kick).
Chicago – McMahon, 2, run (Butler kick).
Chicago – Field goal, 24, Butler.
Chicago – McMahon, 1, run (Butler kick).
Chicago – Phillips, 28, interception return (Butler kick).
Chicago – Perry, 1, run (Butler kick).
New England – Fryar, 8, pass from Grogan (Franklin kick).
Chicago – Safety, Grogan tackled in end zone by Waechter.

Rushing: *Chicago* – Payton, 22 for 61; Suhey, 11 for 52, 1 TD; McMahon, 5 for 14, 2 TD; Thomas, 2 for 8; Gentry, 3 for 15; Perry, 1 for 1, 1 TD; Fuller, 1 for 1; Sanders, 4 for 15. *New England* – C James, 5 for 1; Hawthorne, 1 for –4; Collins, 3 for 4; Weathers, 1 for 3; Grogan, 1 for 3.
Passing: *Chicago* – McMahon, 12 of 20 for 256; Fuller, 0 of 4; Perry, 0 of 0. *New England* – Eason, 0 of 6; Grogan, 17 of 30 for 177, 1 TD, 2 int.
Receiving: *Chicago* – Gault, 4 for 129; Moorehead, 2 for 22; Thomas, 1 for 4; Suhey, 1 for 24; Gentry, 2 for 41; Margerum, 2 for 36. *New England* – Collins, 2 for 19; C James, 1 for 6; Morgan, 7 for 70; Starring, 2 for 39; Ramsey, 2 for 16; Weathers, 1 for 3; Fryar, 2 for 24, 1 TD.
Punting: *Chicago* – Buford, 4 for 43.3 average. *New England* – Camarillo, 6 for 43.8.
Punt Returns: *Chicago* – Ortego, 2 for 20. *New England* – Fryar, 2 for 22.
Kickoff Returns: *Chicago* – Gault, 4 for 49. *New England* – Starring, 7 for 153.
Interceptions: *Chicago* – Phillips, 1 for 18, 1 TD; Morrissey, 1 for 47. *New England* – None.

Super Bowl XX. Chicago reserve CB Reggie Phillips scores on an interception of a pass by Patriot QB Steve Grogan.

PHILLIPS
48

Lest pro football stray too far from its roots with high-tech passing offenses and fancy formations, the game underwent a back-to-the-basics movement in 1985. Nothing could be more fitting than having the NFL's grand old franchise, the Chicago Bears, lead the charge. The basics, of course, were a snarling defense, a stare-in-the-face-of-the-offense mentality, a corps of linebackers, safeties and defensive ends that routinely broke legs, wills, spirits, game plans or anything else that got in the way. Certainly, this defense was paired with a beautifully efficient offense, but make no mistake, the Alpha and Omega of the Bears' success was their defense.

'Defense,' Mike Ditka, the Bears' coach, said. 'You win with defense. I don't think that ever changes. These teams have gotten here because of defense and their ability to create turnovers and to take advantage of them.'

'What their defense does,' Minnesota coach Les Steckel said of the Bears, 'is take the natural reaction out of a football player, based on the multiple looks they give you. They used as many as 14 fronts the other week, when against most teams you look at two or maybe three. So when an offensive lineman sees so many different fronts, instead of just reacting, he has to think, "Am I going to block this way on this play or that way?"'

The Bears, the Super Bowl XX champions, were a curious mix of dastardly characters and sweetly silly stage hounds. The road show was led by William

Opposite top: *Chicago QB Jim McMahon talks with Bear coach Mike Ditka.*

Opposite below: *Chicago DE Richard Dent played a great defensive game and was later named the game's MVP.*

Above: *McMahon fades back. He passed for 256 in the game and rushed for 14 and two TDs.*

Left: *Steve Grogan replaced the ineffective Tony Eason as the Patriot QB early in the game.*

PERRY
72
50

'Refrigerator' Perry, the monstrous defensive tackle and sometimes fullback out of Clemson whose size and gap-toothed grin made him a folk hero and a media-money machine spewing out endorsements with down-home ease. The sensational one was quarterback Jim McMahon, a Brigham Young star whose flamboyance belied the little-believed truth that he was a family man in his private life. His loud mouth irritated coach Mike Ditka, but he had an arm and a knack for winning. So he was tolerated. Then there was the incomparable yardage machine, Walter 'Sweetness' Payton, who had led the NFC five times in rushing since 1977. Other names cropped up with regularity: wide receiver Willie Gault, safety Gary Fencik.

Fortunately, the team had some very bad defenders who tended to be the serious types. Otis Wilson, Mike Singletary and Wilber Marshall were the game's best linebackers. Richard Dent, Steve McMichael and Dan Hampton completed the defensive line. Somehow the team clowns convinced its more respectable members to join a bit of video-age hype called 'The Super Bowl Shuffle.' The video, plus the blizzard of posters, books and other endorsements, all generated huge revenues. Almost as huge as the revenues the Bears generated on the field. They finished the season 15-1 (losing only to Marino and the Dolphins), then chilled the Giants, 21-0, and the Rams, 24-0, in the playoffs.

The New England Patriots of former Baltimore great coach Raymond Berry featured running back Craig James and revolving quarterbacks Steve Grogan and Tony Eason. The Patriots had selected Eason from the University of Illinois in the first round of the 1983 NFL draft. For years, the fiery Grogan had carried the franchise on his arm, but with Eason showing great promise, the veteran quarterback was relegated to backup.

Left: *308-lb Bear DT William 'The Refrigerator' Perry (72) was later inserted at RB. He gained only one yard, a TD.*

Top: *McMahon signals a TD.*

Above: *Patriot coach Raymond Berry.*

Above: *Bear MVP Richard Dent.*

Right: *Patriot LB Steve Nelson runs toward RB Walter Payton. Payton led in rushing with 61.*

Far right: *Patriot starting QB Tony Eason had a poor game, gaining no yards passing or rushing.*

Eason had had his problems over the course of the 1985 season. He had thrown for 2156 yards but struck for only 11 touchdowns against 17 interceptions. Grogan had added another 1311 yards to the air game. But the Patriot strength was their rushing attack. Craig James had run for 1227 yards and Tony Collins for 657 more as the Pats ran up an 11-5 record and made the playoffs as a wild-card team. Their first round victory over the New York Jets wasn't pretty, but it was sufficient, 26-14 to move them into the AFC championship against the Miami Dolphins. There Eason performed with spare but deadly precision. In driving the Patriots to a 31-14 win, he completed 10 of 12 passes for 71 yards and three touchdowns. Prior to that, the Patriots hadn't beaten Miami in the Orange Bowl in 18 years.

The Super Bowl matchup produced few believers in the Patriots. Most observers figured the Bears' defense would eat them alive, and they were right. Sportswriters recognized a sense of purpose among the Bears, particularly Walter Payton, who said, 'A lot of sweat, pain and frustration leads up to this, a lot of Julys and Decembers. And I'm enjoying it. But it's not enough just to be here. We want to win.'

New England linebacker Steve Nelson told reporters, 'The key thing is stopping their running game.' But no one really believed there was a key. Even the Bears made little attempt to mask their lack of respect for the Patriots. 'I feel good,' defensive end Richard Dent said. 'I'm pretty anxious to get it over and put the ring on my finger.'

Instead, the pre-game talk focused on the inane. The handwritten message on McMahon's headband was an item of interest. During the season, he had written the name of the shoe company with which he held a promotional contract and flashed that name for TV cameras. But commissioner Pete Rozelle had forbidden that practice. After that, McMahon had followed with a series of comic messages, leading to speculation as to what he might write for the Super Bowl in New Orleans.

'I don't know what I might put on my headband this time,' Jim McMahon said. 'It might depend on what's going on before the game.' McMahon also drew attention for the acupuncture treatment he received for his bruised buttock. 'I worked hard all year,' said McMahon. 'I missed a couple of games because I wanted to be around for the playoffs. So there's no way I will miss this. But I guess this (the bruised buttock) is news. It's a pain in the butt, really.'

The Chicago coach tried to maintain his seriousness amid that atmosphere. 'I told our players that the Super Bowl game will probably be the biggest game of their life,' said Ditka, and added, 'but it won't be the last game of their life.'

For their part, the Patriots seemed interested in not stirring Ditka and the Bears up too much. 'This week, there'll be a whole lot of words,' coach Berry said, 'and I told my players to be careful because you could drown in 'em.'

Some speculation centered on whether the veteran Grogan would get the starting nod over Eason. 'The

EASON
11
73
67

Left: *Jim McMahon hands off to RB Dennis Gentry. Gentry made only 15 yards rushing, but he received twice for 41, once for a first down on the New England one. (Perry took the ball over for the score.)*

Right: *Bart Starr, Joe Namath and other Hall-of-Famers stand before a statue of the Vince Lombardi Trophy in the opening ceremonies at the Superdome.*

Super Bowl's not a game you come into like a Little League team and say, "Well, we're here to have fun, and we're going to try to play everybody," Grogan said. 'You just don't do that. There's a lot of money at stake and a lot of pride at stake, and nobody's worried about my feelings if I don't get on the field and that doesn't bother me a bit.'

In reality, the Patriots were as worried about the Bears' offense as about their defense. 'What makes the Super Bowl different is Jim McMahon's scrambling ability,' said Jim Carr, the Patriots' secondary coach. 'We're really concerned about things like that.' In the fuss over their great defense, Chicago's prodigious offense had been overlooked. 'That doesn't bother us,' said Jim Covert, Chicago offensive tackle, 'because the defense deserves all the credit it gets. We know what we can do. We've led the league in rushing each year for the last three years. I think that's a pretty good accomplishment. I think we're starting to get maturity. . . . We had a good year this year, but we can play better. The good thing is that we're all young. I think this line is going to be around a long time.'

The weight of the challenge, plus the carnival atmosphere in New Orleans, began to take its toll on the Patriots in the days before the game. Their worst fears would come true that Sunday, when the Bears made a meal of them, turning the game into a 46-10 rout. For some reason, it was the most-watched program, probably because of the Chicago sideshow, in television history. Analyst Dick Vermeil summed up the destruction nicely for reporters: 'The Bears started moving. The Patriots started recognizing they were being embarassed offensively. They weren't making any yards, any first downs. They tried doing things they thought were best and all of a sudden they've got minus 19 yards. The Bears were just dominating. After New England struck for a field goal and a 3-0 lead, Chicago scored 13 points in the first quarter, 10 in the second, 21 in the third, and 2 with a safety in the fourth when all had been reduced to fun and games. The only great catastrophe was the failure of Walton Payton to score after years of working to take his team to the big game.'

'Disappointed?' Payton said when asked about it. 'Yes, I'm disappointed. I feel bad. But that's the way the game goes. There were other games I didn't get into the end zone. But if they're keying on me, and it opens up holes for other people, I don't mind being the rabbit.'

'It's a shame that Walter didn't score a touchdown,' Jim McMahon said. 'But that's not my decision.'

The emphasis remained on the Chicago defense, with defensive end Richard Dent being named the MVP. 'Buddy Ryan,' said Mike Singletary, the Bears' linebacker, 'is the first MVP of our defense. Without him, this wouldn't have happened today.' Ryan, however, had plans to leave the Bears to take the head coaching position with the Philadelphia Eagles.

For Berry, the Hall of Fame receiver for Johnny Unitas in the glory days of the Baltimore Colts, the outcome was a humbling experience. 'If you're in the league long enough, you're going to get your rear handed to you,' Berry said. 'And that's what happened to us today.'

The Bears had their first championship since 1946 and the days of George Halas and Sid Luckman. 'It was a long way, but it was worth it,' Ditka said. 'A lot of dreams were fulfilled. A lot of frustrations have been ended.'

70
53

Super Bowl XXI

New York Giants 39, Denver Broncos 20

25 January 1987
Rose Bowl, Pasedena, Calif.
Attendance: 101,063

Denver	10	0	0	10	—	20
Giants	7	2	17	13	—	39

Denver – Field goal, 48, Karlis.
Giants – Mowatt, 6, pass from Simms (Allegre kick).
Denver – Elway, 4, run (Karlis kick).
Giants – Safety, Elway tackled in end zone by Martin.
Giants – Bavaro, 13, pass from Simms (Allegre kick).
Giants – Field goal, 21, Allegre.
Giants – Morris, 1, run (Allegre kick).
Giants – McConkey, 6, pass from Simms (Allegre kick).
Denver – Field goal, 28, Karlis.
Giants – Anderson, 2, run (kick failed).
Denver – V Johnson, 47, pass from Elway (Karlis kick).

Rushing: *Denver* – Elway, 6 for 27, 1 TD; Willhite, 4 for 19; Sewell, 3 for 4; Lang, 2 for 2; Winder, 4 for 0. *Giants* – Morris, 20 for 67, 1 TD; Simms, 3 for 25; Rouson, 3 for 22; Galbreath, 4 for 17; Carthon, 3 for 4; Anderson, 2 for 1, 1 TD; Rutledge, 3 for 0.
Passing: *Denver* – Elway, 22 of 37 for 304, 1 TD, 1 int.; Kubiak, 4 of 4 for 48. *Giants* – Simms, 22 of 25 for 268, 3 TD.
Receiving: *Denver* – V Johnson, 5 for 121, 1 TD; Willhite, 5 for 39; Winder, 4 for 34; Jackson, 3 for 51; Watson, 2 for 54; Sampson, 2 for 20; Mobley, 2 for 17; Sewell, 2 for 12; Lang, 1 for 4. *Giants* – Bavaro, 4 for 51, 1 TD; Morris, 4 for 20; Carthon, 4 for 13; Robinson, 3 for 62; Manuel, 3 for 4; McConkey, 2 for 50, 1 TD; Rouson, 1 for 23; Mowatt, 1 for 6, 1 TD.
Punting: *Denver* – Horan, 2 for 41.0 average. *Giants* – Landeta, 3 for 46.0 average.
Punt Returns: *Denver* – Willhite, 1 for 9. *Giants* – McConkey, 1 for 25.
Kickoff Returns: *Denver* – Bell, 3 for 48; Lang, 2 for 36. *Giants* – Rouson, 3 for 56; Flynn, 1 for −3.
Interceptions: *Denver* – None. *Giants* – Patterson, 1 for −7.

The New York Giants went into Super Bowl XXI much favored over Denver, but by the half they had a one-point deficit.

GIANTS

Left: *The Giants came to the Super Bowl with an impressive 14-2 season record. They were formidably well balanced in both offense and defense.*

Right: *In the regular season Giant QB Phil Simms had passed for almost 3500 yards.*

Right below: *Giant coach Bill Parcells had to endure a bath of Gatorade every time his team won a game.*

The whole Bears thing seemed a sure fire bet as a repeat championship for 1986, but Jim McMahon's shoulder was injured, and the rest of the team seemed to be tripping over egos distended by all the media attention from their Super Bowl XX victory, Chicago coach Mike Ditka brought in diminutive Boston College Heisman trophy winner Doug Flutie, who had played with the New Jersey Generals of the recently dispatched United States Football League. Flutie struggled, and the Bears rolled over and died under the weight of the Washington Redskins in the playoffs.

The real team of 1986 was the Giants, similar to their predecessors in that when they grinned their defensive grin, the fangs were nasty linebackers. Lawrence Taylor out of the University of North Carolina had shattered Joe Theismann's shin on Monday Night Football during the 1985 season, which added to his already established reputation as the most vicious player in the league.

The New York defense was much, much more, however. Mainly it was armored with great linebackers, notably Harry Carson, Carl Banks, Pepper Johnson and Gary Reasons. The offense wasn't bad either, with little Joe Morris giving coach Bill Parcells a great ground game, and Phil Simms, who overcame fan discontentment to prove he was a great quarterback.

Phil Simms dreamed the great dream of all pro quarterbacks in 1986. He took his team to the Super Bowl, and once there, he put on one of the finest passing performances in the history of the game. In leading the New York Giants to a 39-20 victory over the Denver Broncos in Super Bowl XXI, Simms completed 22 of 25 passes to set a Super Bowl record for completion percentage, a whopping 88.0 (far beyond the 73.5 percent turned in by Cincinnati's Ken Anderson in 1982). Simms' three touchdown passes took the kick out of the Broncos and assured Simms the game MVP trophy.

When the Giants had selected him out of Morehead State in the first round of the 1979 draft, they were a franchise struggling to regain respectability. But coach Ray Perkins tutored his young quarterback and built an offense New York could be proud of. When Perkins left after the 1982 season, coach Bill Parcells stepped in and completed the job.

On occasion, however, the offense had struggled. In 1981 the Giants earned a wild-card playoff spot, but had fallen to last place in their division by 1983. Then for the next two years, Simms rebounded them to wild-card finishes. There were signs along the way he was bringing his game on line. In October 1985, he completed 40 of 62 passes against Cincinnati for 513 yards, the second highest single-game total in the history of the league.

As the team began to emerge, reporters asked Simms if he had been helped by the years of losing. 'You know what it does?' he said. 'It makes you self-doubt everything. If you win a game, you can say, "I

did this, and maybe it helped us win a game." If you lose, you say, "Maybe if I wouldn't have made them, maybe we wouldn't have lost." The self-doubt creeps in, and you're in trouble.'

The New York fans and media had been merciless with Simms at times. 'It's a shame,' said Ron Erhardt, New York's offensive coordinator. 'I think most of the fans think he's a pretty good quarterback. In the past, the boo-birds were wrong.'

Then in 1986 came the banner season. Simms passed for nearly 3500 yards, Morris rushed for more than 1500 and tight end Mark Bavaro caught 66 passes for 1001 yards as the Giants left opponents in their wake on the way to a 14-2 regular-season finish.

The season became marked by icy Gatorade baths the Giants' players administered to Parcells after each victory. Nose tackle Jim Burt was pinpointed as the culprit who first dumped a cooler of green juice on Parcells' head. 'We were playing Washington, which had been to the Super Bowl two years in a row,' Burt said. 'It was a crossroads game for us. Bill had been on me all week, ticking me off. So near the end of the game, I decided to get him. I dumped Gatorade all over him. The guys stood around with their mouths open.'

Dripping with Gatorade, the Giants shoved their way into the playoffs where they put on the most brutal display of power ever witnessed in pro football history. In the first round the Giants smashed Joe Montana and the San Francisco 49ers, 49-3, as Morris rushed for 159 yards. In the NFC championship game, they chilled the Washington Redskins, 17-0,

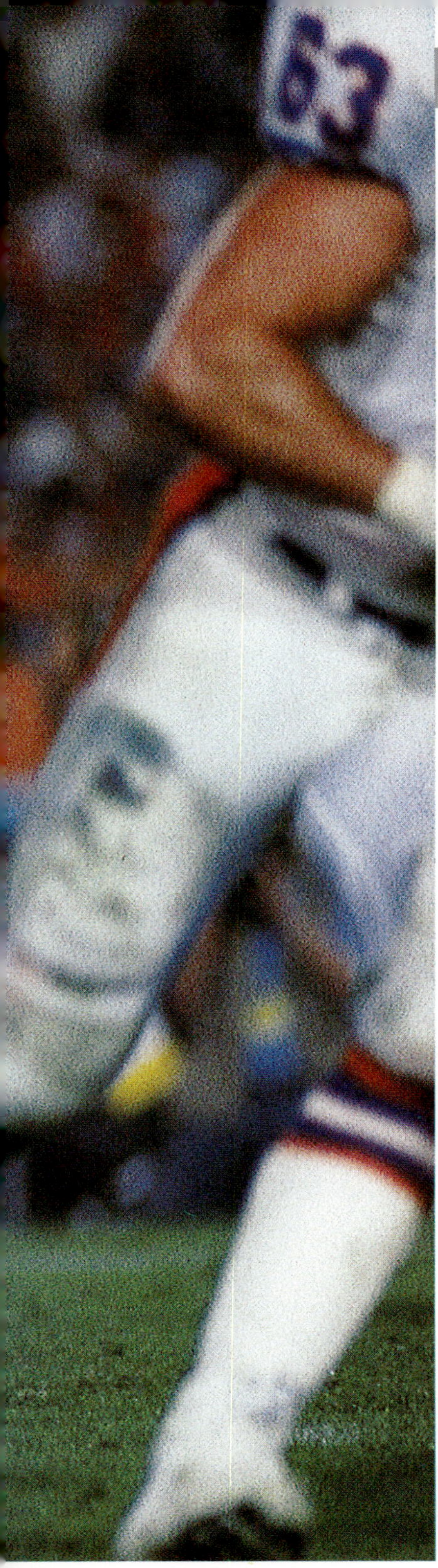

Left: *Running back-cum-wide receiver Steve Sewell was one of the Bronco's aces.*

Right: *Denver QB John Elway had a regular season about as good as Simms', passing for 3485 yards and 19 TDs.*

Right below: *Thanks to Bernie Kosar and the Cleveland Browns Denver almost didn't make it to Super Bowl XXI. The AFC championship was decided in overtime, 23-20, by a Bronco field goal.*

and immediately sharpened their fangs for Super Bowl XXI in Pasedena.

The AFC survivor had been the Denver Broncos, led by John Elway. They had won the AFC Western Division with an 11-5 record, then found some magic in the playoffs.

When Elway came out of Stanford University in 1983, the book on him had cited boundless talent but had questioned his moxie and consistency. His first four years with the Denver Broncos seemed to confirm that assessment. Then with the 1986 season, Elway silenced his questioners. In the process, he contributed a great moment or two to the annals of the game.

The regular season went nicely enough. Elway completed 280 of 504 attempts for 3485 yards and 19

touchdowns against 13 interceptions. In the playoffs, the Broncos fell behind New England, but Elway rallied them for a 22-17 win to advance to the AFC finals against the Browns. Cleveland had reached the finals with a dramatic overtime win over the New York Jets.

The victory capped a special season for the Browns, and the bleacher fans in Cleveland Stadium had come to be known as the Dawgs for all their yelping and barking in delight at the team's resurgence. Elway was hampered by an injured left ankle, and the Broncos seemed to draw on that image, limping step for step with the Browns through the chilly afternoon to a 13-13 tie in the fourth quarter. Then with just under six minutes left, Cleveland quarterback Bernie Kosar passed to wide receiver Brian Brennan, who stepped around safety Dennis Smith and ran jubilantly to the end zone. The play covered 48 yards and gave the Browns what seemed to be an insurmountable lead, 20-13.

The lead seemed even more insurmountable on the ensuing kickoff when the Broncos bobbled the ball and wound up on their own two-yard line, first and forever with 5:32 left. Elway huddled his team in the end zone as the Dawgs pelted the proceedings with dog biscuits. Elway smiled and told his mates, 'If you work hard, good things are going to happen.'

He created some working room with a short pass to receiver Sammy Winder, then Elway ran for 11 yards and a first down. Next he spun one 22 yards to Steve Sewell. Steve Watson caught the next one for 12 yards. Presto, the Broncos were poised at the Brown 40-yard line with the clock showing 1:59, and the Dawgs' yelping was rising in pitch to a long, low hangdog howl. Their growl came back with a snap when Elway threw an incompletion and was sacked on the next play for an eight-yard loss. But Elway dropped to the shotgun, managed to control a bumbled snap and zipped the ball to Mark Jackson for a 20-yard gain to the Cleveland 28. Elway's next shot, a 14-yarder to Sewell, was followed by an incompletion. So Elway broke and ran for nine yards to the five. There, on third and one he burned a fastball into Jackson's tummy for the touchdown. Rich Karlis' placement tied it at 20.

When Cleveland stalled in overtime, Elway once more jumpstarted the Broncos and drove them down to the Brown 15, where Karlis punched up the game-winning field goal, 23-20. It was a great win for Denver coach Dan Reeves, but he had little time to savor it with the Giants waiting in his team's path.

'I hope the game is not one-sided,' said Reeves. 'If it isn't, we have a chance to win it. I think one of the keys for the Giants is to stay on the field with their offense and keep John Elway off the field. You don't stop Lawrence Taylor; you hope you slow him down.'

Left: *Giant RB Joe Morris carries on a handoff from Simms. 44 is RB Maurice Carthon.*

Top: *John Elway gets set. He had a fine first half. In all he passed for 304 yards.*

Above: *New York Giants coach Bill Parcells.*

'Years ago, in college,' said Parcells, 'the Lawrence Taylors would have been playing offense. When the college went to two platoons, they took the guys like Lawrence who could really run and made them full-backs and tight ends. Now, almost all the big guys in college are linemen and all the fast guys are on defense.' Yet in other seasons the Giants' defense was well known. The difference for 1986 had been the development of the offense, particularly the ground game with Joe Morris. 'Morris has become one of the best in the league at finding cracks in the defense,' said Joe Collier, the Broncos' defensive coordinator, 'and exploiting 'em and popping through 'em. So you can't concentrate on just the passing game. You used to be able to load up against the Giants, and the passing attack. Morris makes the defense stay honest.'

Sensing the Giants' balance, the oddsmakers had installed them as a 9 to 10 point favorite. 'We knew what to expect,' Elway said of the spread. 'But we don't plan on giving the Giants any points just because they're favored. It'll be a zero-zero game when it starts.'

As for the Giants, the news of the spread only added to their considerable confidence. 'I'm comfortable being the favorite,' said center Bart Oates. 'I should be comfortable because we're going to win. But being the favorite doesn't necessarily mean we're the better team.' Coach Reeves was a bit envious of the Giants'

Left: *Simms gets off a close one. He completed 22 of 25 for a Super Bowl record of 88 percent and was the game MVP.*

Below: *Giants Phil McConkey (80) and Mark Bavaro (89) hug in celebration.*

Right: *Elway searches for a receiver as Giant LB Lawrence Taylor closes in.*

position and admitted it to sportswriters: 'I wish I was favored by 10 and I just finished beating two teams by 66-3. I would like teams to fear us. I would like them to come into Mile High Stadium and fear us like they feared the Giants this season.'

The oddsmakers were left to do a bit of squirming in the first half. In the opening drive, Denver went 45 yards and struck on a Rich Karlis field goal. Then Simms put the Giants on top with a six-yard touchdown pass. Denver came right back with a strong return by Ken Bell, which led to a touchdown drive. Harry Carson was called for a late hit that helped the effort as Elway completed the damage with a four-yard quarterback draw up the middle for a 10-7 lead. They obviously had the momentum, but watched it begin to slip away when Karlis missed a 23-yard field goal.

Leonard Marshall sacked Elway in the second quarter, and Karlis missed another field goal just before the half, leaving the score at 10-9. 'I hurt our momentum,' Rich Karlis said of the two kicks. 'The snap was good, the hold was good, everything was good. I feel like I let everybody down. We didn't want to waste many opportunities today, but I did.'

The Giants really came alive at the outset of the second half, putting 17 points on the scoreboard in the third quarter, then 13 in the fourth. The Broncos finally scored 10 in the fourth, but that did little more than ease the pain of the rout.

'We knew going into the ball game,' a disappointed Reeves said afterward, 'that if we didn't take advantage of every opportunity we had, we would be in tough shape.'

'Now,' said Lawrence Taylor, 'no matter what people say about our team, whether the Giants don't look good anymore or whatever, as long as I live I'll always have a Super Bowl ring. One time in my career, we are considered the best in the world. That

was the most important thing. This has been a long time coming,' he said. 'I just wish I didn't have to wait so long.' The MVP Award was the ideal salve for the years that Simms had endured the boos in New York. 'They [the Broncos] showed no respect. I'm not taking anything away from them. But they showed us no respect throwing the ball. We were going to make them show us some today. You can't be a top quarterback in this league unless you have a top team.'

7
TAYLOR
56

BRANCH

Super Bowl XXII

Washington Redskins 42, Denver Broncos 10

31 January 1988
Jack Murphy Stadium, San Diego
Attendance: 73,302

Washington	0	35	0	7	—	42
Denver	10	0	0	0	—	10

Denver – Nattiel, 56, pass from Elway (Karlis kick).
Denver – Field goal, 24, Karlis.
Washington – Sanders, 80, pass from Williams (Haji-Sheikh kick).
Washington – G Clark, 27, pass from Williams (Haji-Sheikh kick).
Washington – T Smith, 58, run (Haji-Sheikh kick).
Washington – Sanders, 50, pass from Williams (Haji-Sheikh kick).
Washington – Didier, 8, pass from Williams (Haji-Sheikh kick).
Washington – T Smith, 4, run (Haji-Sheikh kick).

Rushing: *Washington* – T Smith, 22 for 204, 2 TD; Bryant, 8 for 38; G Clark, 1 for 25; Rogers, 5 for 17; Griffin, 1 for 2; Williams, 2 for –2; Sanders, 1 for –4. *Denver* – Lang, 5 for 38; Elway, 3 for 32; Winder, 8 for 30; Sewell, 1 for –3.
Passing: *Washington* – Williams, 18 of 29 for 340, 4 TD, 1 int.; Schroeder, 0 for 1. *Denver* – Elway, 14 of 38 for 257, 1 TD, 1 int.; Sewell, 1 of 1 for 23.
Receiving: *Washington* – Sanders, 9 for 193, 2 TD; G Clark, 3 for 55, 1 TD; Warren, 2 for 15; Monk, 1 for 40; Bryant, 1 for 20; T Smith, 1 for 9; Didier, 1 for 8, 1 TD. *Denver* – Jackson, 4 for 76; Sewell, 4 for 41; Nattiel, 2 for 69, 1 TD; Kay, 2 for 38; Winder, 1 for 26; Elway, 1 for 23; Lang, 1 for 7.
Punting: *Washington* – Cox, 4 for 37.5 average. *Denver* – Horan, 7 for 36.1 average.
K Punt Returns: *Washington* – Green, 1 for 0. *Denver* – K Clark, 2 for 18.
Kickoff Returns: *Washington* – Sanders, 3 for 46. *Denver* – Bell, 5 for 88.
Interceptions: *Washington* – Wilburn, 2 for 11; Davis, 1 for 0. *Denver* – Castille, 1 for 0.

Super Bowl XXII. Redskin WR Ricky Sanders takes off. He caught nine for a remarkable 193 and two TDs.

It seems strange that in a season of unfulfilled dreams, the football world would hold to a naive hope that Super Bowl XXII would unfold as an exhilarating event, that the Denver Broncos and Washington Redskins would provide a classic pro shootout, that finally the Super Bowl of the 1980s would live up to its name.

Of course, it didn't happen. Those high hopes were lost on the loose turf of San Diego Jack Murphy Stadium. The Redskins beat Denver, 42-10, to win their second title in six years. With the two teams struggling in a death match, Washington dashed the Broncos with an astounding outburst of offense in the second quarter. Just the same, it's not quite possible to dismiss the 1987 season and Super Bowl XXII as a blowout. If nothing else, the proceedings offered a fresh unpredictability. And if the NFL had been anything in the previous two seasons, it was predictable. In 1985 the Chicago Bears were obviously the dominant team. Ditto for the New York Giants in 1986. But the Skins in '87? Few people believed they had the snap and finger pop to dance the big dance.

Left: *Doug Williams was coach Joe Gibbs' choice as starting QB for the Skins. His backup, Jay Schroeder, was also well qualified.*

Right: *Washington cornerback Darrell Green rams Bronco WR Mark Jackson out of play on the sidelines.*

Right below: *John Elway again quarterbacked for Denver. He passed for 257 and one TD in the game but completed only 14 of 38 and was intercepted three times and sacked five.*

Then again, 1987 was a strike year, setting the entire league spinning into an atmosphere of uncertainty. If you remember, Washington also had thrived in the strike season of 1982, when play was stopped for seven weeks, thus reducing the regular season from 16 to nine games. Once play resumed, the Redskins had gathered momentum to bully their way past Miami in Super Bowl XVII.

In 1987 strike was different in that the owners decided to field replacement teams rather than lose money while waiting the players out. Fearing trouble would come when the players' union contract expired in September, some owners had begun lining up non-union replacement players early in the pre-season. When the National Football League Players Association announced its strike in September, the league quickly assembled new teams and missed only one game.

The action brought cries of 'scabs' from the union and hard feelings on all sides, but it was effective. For three weeks, the NFL took on the air of the old AFL, with a mix of young, unproven talent and old second-chancers getting a shot at playing in the league. A few at a time, the striking players broke ranks and returned to their teams. Rather than face a rout, the uinion sent its members back to work after the second week of games. But the owners decided the players hadn't returned early enough, and as if to prove a point, they held the regulars out a third week while the replacements took one last dream fling with the NFL.

By far, the most interesting team during this period was the Washington Redskins, where coach Joe Gibbs assembled a roster of replacements that won all three games. Even better, none of the striking regular Redskins broke ranks and returned early. Whereas many other NFL teams were torn by the conflicts of the strike, the Redskins returned as a unified team. Yet they weren't without their problems. Starting quarterback Jay Schroeder played inconsistently and was replaced by veteran backup Doug Williams. Williams played with the promise he had shown in early stints with Tampa Bay of the NFL and the Arizona Outlaws of the defunct United States Football League. When Williams sustained a back injury in practice, Schroeder returned to the starting lineup and played well, hurling three touchdown passes to lead a comeback over the New York Giants. Once Williams returned, Gibbs was faced with a difficult choice between his quarterbacks, and Gibbs' choice was Williams. The rest, as they say, is history.

The foul air of the strike dissipated with amazing rapidity once the schedule resumed. With coach Jim Mora leading, the New Orleans Saints charged to the first winning season and playoff berth in the team's

history. But San Francisco and Chicago finished atop the NFC and claimed a home-field advantage in the playoffs. Some advantage.

The playoffs opened with Minnesota playing at New Orleans, where the Saints were heavily favored. The Vikings dashed them, 44-10. From there, Minnesota moved to a showdown at San Francisco, the team considered the favorite to take it all. But once again the 49ers drooped in the playoffs, and Minnesota came away with an overwhelming victory, keyed by Anthony Carter's playoff record 227 yards receiving.

Meanwhile, the Redskins traveled to the cold of Chicago to play the Bears, the team they had upset in the playoffs the year before. With Jim McMahon returning from injury, the Bears took a 14-0 lead as Williams struggled at quarterback for Washington. He did, however, uincork enough big plays to even

Above: *Denver WR Ricky Nattiel made the game's first TD.*

Right: *End Dexter Manley (72) predicted a Skins victory.*

Far right: *Kicker Rich Karlis made Denver's second score.*

the score at 14. Then Redskin defensive speedster Darrell Green produced a spectacular punt return, highlighted by his hurdling a would-be tackler, to score Washington's winning points, 21-14.

The wild-card Vikings hit the road once more, this time to Washington, where the Redskins prevailed, 17-10, as Green broke up a last-second pass play at the Washington goal. For the third time in six years, Joe Gibbs was taking a team to the Super Bowl.

Over in the AFC, Denver coach Dan Reeves was heading his Broncos toward a repeat appearance in

the Super Bowl, by much the same arduous route as in 1986. Houston had made a surprise appearance in the playoffs, then beat Seattle, 23-20, in overtime to become the Broncos' first playoff opponent. Denver promptly trounced Houston and returned again to the AFC title game. Their opponents in the overtime thriller the year before, Bernie Kosar and the Cleveland Browns, were determined to get another shot at the Super Bowl. Led by Earnest Byner's 122 yards rushing, the Browns returned to the AFC title game by downing the Indianapolis Colts and Eric Dickerson (the Colts had acquired the league's star runner in a trade with the Rams). Cleveland fans were primed for their beloved Browns to invade Denver's Mile High Stadium and come away with the AFC title. But Kosar and the Browns fell way behind in the first half, only to rally incredibly in the final two quarters. Trailing 38-31 in the dying minutes, Kosar raced the Browns downfield, where Byner was stripped of the ball just as he broke into the end zone for the tying touchdown. The Broncos recovered the fumble and averted an overtime. For the second year in a row, the Browns had to swallow their disappointment as Denver advanced.

The Broncos were installed as a three-and-a-half point favorite amid speculation that Washinton and Denver would bring some excitement to the Super Bowl. 'As hard as you try as coaches, it seems like the [Super Bowl] games haven't been that exciting,' Reeves conceded to reporters in the days before the game. 'I'm not saying that this one will [be close], but if you look at how we've been in every game over the last few years, and the Redskins are always in the game, hopefully we'll have one of those matchups that people have been dreaming about.'

Much of the pre-game hype focused on Denver quarterback John Elway, who had been lauded as one of the game's greatest, and his three receivers, Ricky Nattiel, Mark Jackson and Vance Johnson, nicknamed 'the Three Amigos' after the comic movie by the same name. Washington quarterback Doug Williams, on the other hand, was considered suspect because he had struggled with the Tampa Bay Buccaneers in the NFC title game earlier in his career. It was implied that Williams had failed to perform in the big game. For the most part, Washington players bore this affrontery to their quarterback and team in silence, except for their outspoken defensive end. Dexter Manley, who told reporters, 'You all who picked Denver are going to be very upset because we're going to win.' In truth, no one felt secure about the outcome. The last time the teams had played, in late 1986, the Broncos had won a wild one, 31-30. If nothing else, a high score seemed likely.

'I think it's possible a lot of points will be put on the board,' Reeves said.

'I look for a wide open game,' said Richie Petitbon, Washington's assistant head coach/defense. 'Every down is going to be like third down.' The insiders, however, knew Washington's defensive line was large, swift and talented. And their offense had explosive potential. The ground game ran a multi-faceted counter trap that usually seemed to work behind Washington's large offensive line.

'We've got to shut down that counter running play they've been using for years,' said Denver linebacker Karl Mecklenburg. 'Their tight ends don't make that much difference on pass coverages. As far as running goes, they don't declare a strong side, so you can't determine which way they're going to run easily.' Mecklenburg's concerns would prove well-founded, although in the early going the game appeared to be a Bronco blowout. In the loose soil, the Redskins had severe trouble getting their offense going, or for that matter returning a kickoff to their 20. Denver, meanwhile, came out with a high energy level, with the Bronco defense holding Washington on the first series. Then Elway struck on Denver's first offensive play, lofting the ball to rookie sensation Ricky Nattiel, who had run past Redskin cornerback Barry Wilburn, for a 56-yard touchdown pass.

The next time they got the ball, the Broncos drove 60 yards in seven plays and appeared on the verge of taking a big lead. But a quarterback draw failed, and Rich Karlis knocked up a 24-yard field goal for a 10-0 lead. In the 21 previous Super Bowls, no team had ever come back from such a deficit. Things seemed even darker for Washington when receiver Ricky Sanders fumbled the ensuing kickoff, but the Redskins recovered. Then later in the period, Williams twisted his knee and had to be replaced for one series by Schroeder, who threw an incompletion and was sacked.

But the Redskin miseries miraculously died with the first-period clock, as Williams returned to the game and directed one of the most amazing reversals since the New York Giants surprised the Chicago Bears in the famous 'Sneakers Game,' the 1934 NFL championship. Trailing the Bears, 13-3, while playing on the frozen field of the Polo Grounds, the Giants had switched to rubber-soled shoes at halftime, helping them to erupt for 27 fourth-quarter points to win, 30-13. The Redskins' turnaround also involved a shoe change. Finding their footing in short cleats was troublesome on the loose turf. So many of the players switched to longer cleats and suddenly both Washington's offense and defense got traction.

Yet Washington's second-quarter performance was much more than footing. Williams opened with an 80-yard TD bomb to Sanders over Denver cornerback Mark Haynes. About a minute later, Washington got the ball back and Williams drove the Redskins to a 14-10 lead with a second touchdown, this time a 28-yard scoring pass to receiver Gary Clark. Denver answered with a 54-yard drive to the Washington 26, but Karlis missed a 43-yard field goal. Little did anyone think that series would be Denver's last hurrah. Two plays later, Washington's rookie running back Timmy Smith, a surprise starter in place of George Rogers, broke outside on the counter trap play for a 58-yard touchdown run and a 21-10 lead.

Williams followed that moments later with another touchdown pass, 50 yards to Sanders, and the lead was 28-10. Before the half, he threw his fourth TD pass, the last one going eight yards to tight end Clint Didier for a 35-10 lead. On the quarter, Williams had completed 9 of 11 attempts for 228 yards and four touchdowns. For the quarter, Washington had racked up an astounding 356 yards in total offense. The Redskins had scored a record 35 points while possessing the ball for only 5:54 of the quarter.

A second-half touchdown run by Smith closed out the scoring, and from there the chore became tabulating the records, including a Super Bowl record 340 yards passing by Williams, a Super Bowl record 204 yards rushing by Smith, much of it coming on the

Above: *Doug Williams, down but not seriously hurt. The Skins QB passed for a Super Bowl record of 340 yards. He was, deservedly, the game MVP.*

Left: *Rookie RB Timmy Smith made two Washington TDs, one on a 58-yard run.*

Right: *Williams gets one off easily before Bronco DE Rulon Jones can reach him.*

counter trap play, a Super Bowl record 193 yards receiving by Sanders, and a Super Bowl record of 602 yards total offense by Washington. It was the biggest comeback in Super Bowl history. 'The thing about our team that we never got any credit for was that all year, when we got behind, we never let down,' Williams commented after the game.

'We felt that no matter what the score, we've just got to do our thing,' said Joe Bugel, Washington's assistant head coach/offense. 'We've been catching up all year. Our players don't panic being down.'

The Denver coaches, players and their fans had experienced the supreme football roller coaster ride, soaring to the lead in one quarter, plummeting to a loss the next. 'I'm hurt and embarrassed,' linebacker Karl Mecklenburg said.

'We needed to get the ball and get some momentum and we never did that,' said Elway, who completed 14 of 38 passes for 247 yards and a touchdown, was intercepted three times (twice by Barry Wilburn) and sacked five times. Williams, meanwhile, was voted the game's Most Valuable Player. 'I didn't come here to showcase for the black quarterback,' said Williams. 'I came here to win the Super Bowl.'

Commenting about the game's momentum and Williams' performance, Bronco linebacker Jim Ryan said, 'When he got hurt and came back in, that was a rallying point. They have so much confidence in him.'

Left: *Elway gets set while RB Tony Boddie blocks.*

Above: *Williams said later, 'I didn't come here to showcase for the black quarterback; I came to win the Super Bowl.'*

'He was simply superb after a slow start,' Redskins coach Joe Gibbs said of Williams. 'It certainly was the best I've seen him. I hope this does a lot to make people look at people as players, not as color.'

Another round of praise went to the rookie, Tim Smith, and Washington's fine offensive line, who ran the counter to perfection. 'In high school, I guess my biggest game was about 315 yards. But I'll never forget this one,' said Smith, who erased the Super Bowl mark of 191 rushing yards by Allen for the Los Angeles Raiders in Super Bowl XVIII against the Redskins.

Receiver Ricky Sanders, who had been a star in the United States Football League before coming to the Redskins, was thrust from the shadows to the spotlight that the Three Amigos had occupied before the game. 'I never dreamed it. All your life you always want to have something like this, watching the guys like Lynn Swann,' said Sanders, who broke the single-game Super Bowl record for receiving yards, 161 by Swann of Pittsburgh Steelers.

'We couldn't stop them,' said coach Reeves, confirming the obvious. 'It would have been difficult for anyone to beat the Redskins today. They're definitely the world champions.'

'It snowballed on us,' said Elway, who accepted more than his share of the blame. 'By not getting some points and slowing them down it hurt us. That was the most disappointing thing. We never answered the bell in that second quarter.' Perhaps it wouldn't have done any good to answer that second quarter bell, anyway. It tolled for the Broncos.

Index

(Numerals in italics indicate illustrations)

Index

Picture credits
Special thanks to Focus on Sports, who supplied all the illustrations for this book except for the following:

UPI/Bettmann Newsphotos: pages 8-9(both), 12-13(all three), 16-17(all three), 20-21(all five), 24-25(all six), 28-29(all four), 32-33(all four), 36(upper right), 37(upper left), 41(top), 49(both), 95(upper right), 135(lower left), 145(upper right).

Acknowledgments
The author and publisher would like to thank the following people who helped in the preparation of this book: Barbara Thrasher and John Kirk, who edited it; Mike Rose, who designed it; Lynn Leedy, who did the picture research; and Florence Norton, who prepared the index.